PLANET EARTH AND THE DESIGN HYPOTHESIS

David A. J. Seargent

Hamilton Books
A member of
The Rowman & Littlefield Publishing Group
Lanham · Boulder · New York · Toronto · Plymouth, UK

Copyright © 2007 by
Hamilton Books
4501 Forbes Boulevard
Suite 200
Lanham, Maryland 20706
Hamilton Books Acquisitions Department (301) 459-3366

Estover Road
Plymouth PL6 7PY
United Kingdom

All rights reserved
Printed in the United States of America
British Library Cataloging in Publication Information Available

Library of Congress Control Number: 2007924593
ISBN-13: 978-0-7618-3755-8 (paperback : alk. paper)
ISBN-10: 0-7618-3755-8 (paperback : alk. paper)

∞™ The paper used in this publication meets the minimum
requirements of American National Standard for Information
Sciences—Permanence of Paper for Printed Library Materials,
ANSI Z39.48—1984

For Meg, my wife and best friend

and

to the memory of Barry Austen

Contents

Preface	vii
Acknowledgments	xi

Chapter 1 Anomalous Earth? 1
    What About the Copernican Principle? 4
        An important aside 5
        The Anthropic Principle 6
        The Perfect Cosmological Principle 12
    Our 'Special' Planet 14
        A peculiar planet! 15

Chapter 2 Signs of Design? 33
    Transitive Complexity 39
        TC and information transfer in codes 45
        DNA and the code of life 48
    Evidence of Design? 53
        Life in a 'megaverse'? 55

Chapter 3 Our Privileged Planet 63
    The Privileged Planet Hypothesis 63
        'Perfect' solar eclipses 63
        Measurability, habitability and the chemistry of life 69
        Earthquakes and magnetic fields 75
        Sundry interesting 'coincidences' 77

Chapter 4 A World of Beauty and Awe   87
    Total solar eclipses   93
    Comets, meteors and meteorites   93
    Supernovas   96
    Aurora   96
    Rainbows   97
    A miscellany of beauty and awe   97
  The Secret Beauty of Creation   99
    Cosmic beauty; cosmic awe   99
  Our Place in the World   103
  Possible Misunderstanding of this Position   105

Appendix I   The Sensus Divinatis   111

Appendix II Transitive Complexity and Intentionality   115

Index   121

About the Author   127

Preface

Imagine a child of a very wealthy and insular family. Picture this child being raised under such privileged conditions that no care or comfort is ever wanting. If the child craves attention, a butler or some other servant is instantly at his call. Food is never short. Toys are never withheld. Life is a young child's heaven!

We may well fear that such a child will mature into a selfish and indulgent adult, but that it not our present concern. Rather, we are more interested in the sort of opinion that this child might develop about what it is like to grow up in a normal household. Because, from that child's point of view, the conditions under which he is growing up *are* normal! This is the only life he knows and, from his limited and insular point of view, he assumes that every other child on the planet experiences the same sort of childhood as he!

What a profound shock awaits him when, in the course of time, he ventures forth into the wider world and sees firsthand how anomalous his own childhood has been! His assumption that every human being in the world was raised with the same privileges as he knew will be rocked to the foundation and he will find, to his intense surprise, that what he had always assumed as a normal existence is in fact shared by only an infinitesimal percentage of the human race.

Does such a child exists?

Yes. *We* are the child!

We – the human race – have grown up on a planet abounding in life. We have taken for granted that life of one kind or another adapts to just about every conceivable environment of this world. We look up through the clear atmosphere at the wider universe and, little by little over centuries of scientific endeavor, have come to form a concept of this wider environment and our physical location within it. We see the beauty of the rainbow and marvel at the wonder of the aurora. We stand in awe of the power of a thunderstorm or a volcanic eruption.

And we take it all for granted!

We have long assumed our home planet to be typical of all worlds, just as the rich and insular child thought of his home as just a normal household. We assumed that the processes enabling life to flourish on Earth could be found anywhere in the universe. We seldom gave a second thought to the possibility that the ability to learn about our wider environment was in any sense strange. Nor did we think it unusual that phenomena of great beauty and awe should confront us on this planet.

But, like the child, we eventually reached the age where the wider world could be ignored no longer. And like that child, our early experience of that wider environment came as a rude awakening. The wider world, by and large, lacks the privileges that he had taken for granted. Equally, we see that the wider universe lacks the privileges that we came to regard as normal. The growing child found that he had been raised in a privileged home. We find that we have been raised on a privileged planet.

Planet Earth, I will argue in the following pages, is 'privileged' be being anomalous in a number of ways. It is argued that a number of anomalies – some intrinsic to the planet itself, others extrinsic and belonging to our home world's cosmic environment – conspire to render Earth abnormally habitable.

Some see in this the hand of a Designing Intelligence. Yet, while this is certainly a viable explanation, the mere fact that an improbable combination of anomalies should render our planet habitable is not, by itself, sufficient ground for such a conclusion. If life (or, at the very least, sentient life) requires an environment delicately balanced by the rare combination of a set of improbable anomalies, our very presence indicates *a posteriori* that such a combination has occurred on the planet we occupy. This says nothing, however, as to how this came about. It may indeed be true that the combination of anomalies was deliberately contrived by a superior intellect for the express purpose of enabling our existence, but that is not a necessary conclusion. The skeptic will say that it is just a cosmic fluke. In making an intellectual leap from Earth's habitability to the postulation of a designer, we may be committing the same error as the child who marvels that there is always just enough news to fill the daily newspaper!

If we are to take the Design Hypothesis seriously, we must first of all try to define some characteristic of design. We must, that is to say, determine the manner in which states of affairs that we recognize as intelligently designed differ from those that are not. Then, having isolated this principle characteristic, we re-examine the anomalous nature of Earth to see whether this design characteristic is present.

In the course of this, we highlight, not simply our planet's suitability for life, but also its amazing suitability as a window through which the wider universe can be known and through which the beauty of nature is displayed. This aspect of our planet (though often overlooked) enables humankind to fulfill its thirst for knowledge and its appreciation of beauty in a manner which is quite uncanny. So uncanny indeed, as to suggest the characteristic of Intelligent Design for which we seek!

The arguments of this book are presented as an outline for future discussion rather than as a completed work. While I am aware that the conclusions reached will be welcomed by some and strongly opposed by others, I simply ask that the arguments be followed with an open mind. Many years of prejudice about the 'non-anomalous' nature of Earth has elevated this simple working assumption to the level of *a priori* truth, and it is not easy to disentangle our minds from this dogma. Yet, whether it is admitted or not, advances in knowledge of the universe have reached the stage where this working assumption must be discarded, as many working assumptions sooner or later must. The shift in thinking involved is not easy, but once it is made, a deeper appreciation of our place in the universe opens before us.

If the argument of these pages is correct, the implications are profound. We have long been taught that the human race is nothing more than a cosmic accident, that ours is nothing but a purposeless existence in a purposeless cosmos. If that is true, any meaning we find in life must necessarily be of our own making and confined to the short term. In the long term, there will be no long term.

Can it by coincidental that so many in recent generations appear lost and adrift in the world? If we are constantly being told that life is without purpose, can anyone be blamed for acting according to this belief?

If this view of the universe and life is correct, we had better enjoy the moment, as the writer of *Ecclesiastes* taught long ago. But if it is not correct – if there really is a cosmic design which somehow involves us as sentient creatures on this planet – it is vitally important to recognize this and readjust our thinking. How we perceive our place in the universe greatly affects how we perceive ourselves, and how we perceive ourselves must surely influence our behavior at some level. In view of this, the Design Hypothesis emerges as far more than a mere intellectual exercise.

May this book play some role, how ever minor, in this continuing debate.

David A. J. Seargent
The Entrance
September, 2006

Acknowledgments

In the writing of any work of this nature, many ideas that have been absorbed at one time or another are processed and reproduced, but it would take a memory greater than mine to recall their provenance. Accordingly, I first of all would like to extend my thanks far and wide to anyone whose influence contributed to the chain of thoughts that led to the present book!

In particular though, I would like to thank Damien Spillane, with whom I worked on an initial presentation of what might be called the 'Argument from Beauty and Awe' that occupies an important place in this book. I am greatly indebted to his input and assistance but I especially have him to thank for drawing attention to the subject presented in Appendix One of this book. I should mention that I relegated this to an appendix, not because it is unimportant, but because I sensed when trying to come to grips with this issue that I was standing on the banks of a river having many tributaries, most of which wind through country beyond the parameters of the present book and the competence of its author. It is hoped that others more instructed in such matters will take up the challenges that I can only indicate.

Finally, I would like to thank my wife Meg and others off whom I bounced ideas as the subject matter of this book took shape, for the kind assistance and encouragement of Dr. Mark Fitzmaurice, Mr. Bill Hodgson and all those involved in its production.

Chapter 1
Anomalous Earth?

About fifty years ago, hardly a long time in the history of human thought, some person or group whose name escapes me, published a paperback of pulp-magazine appearance dealing with the question of life on the other planets of our Solar System. Of course, a book of that format may be expected to follow a more sensationalist line than that of an academic tome. This expectation was not disappointed! Nevertheless, the thesis of the book gave a pretty fair indication of the popular thinking of the day and, although the great majority of professional scientists would certainly have been more cautious in their language, not many would have dismissed its content as being totally beyond the pale.

The book's underlying assumption was that some, possibly most, of Earth's planetary neighbors were homes to some form of life. In its more extravagantly speculative pages, this life was pictured as being intelligent. Somewhere the statement was made that when "sober scientific speculation" was applied to the subject, the conclusion was reached that "creatures beyond our wildest imaginings" really may inhabit the worlds around us. There then followed descriptions of the Mercury Lichen Eater, a gorilla-like Venusian who "prowled for food" across the plains of that planet, the Mars Man (a small pixy-like creature with flaring nostrils suited to breathing thin air, shown holding a small telescope in his hands with an observatory dome or some similar structure in the Martian background) and strange creatures with large mule ears and antennae projecting from their foreheads (in lieu of eyes) that may be found lurking on the dark and sunless surface of the planet Jupiter.

All of these creatures paraded before the reader in quite logical presentations. Each was described on the authority of "one scientist" or of "another expert" whose names, curiously, remained unmentioned.

Of course, these views were rather extreme. But, they were extreme in the sense of being on the far end of a spectrum of ideas that were acceptable; even, in the opinion of many laypeople, self-evidently true. Surely, there was life on at least some of the other planets of the Solar System!

Few doubted that Mars, at least, harbored some form of life, although by the 1950s fewer professional scientists were as confident as an earlier generation that this life was intelligent.

Yet, as space became more accessible, either directly through spaceships and automated probes, or indirectly through advances in telescope size and sensitivity, imaging techniques and space-based astronomical instruments, the assumptions that had made extraterrestrial life appear certain, began to change. In a manner that nobody had foreseen, our attitude toward Earth and the other Solar System bodies changed beyond recognition.

Prior to receiving the first pictures from the surface of another world, the human imagination spontaneously pictured our neighboring orbs as 'Never Lands', worlds of fantasy and exotic landscapes where equally exotic creatures seemed quite at home. Those born after the beginning of the space age must find it strange to look back on pre-space-age books depicting a lunar landscape of high jagged peaks and gaping sharp-rimmed craters, or those Walt Disney speculations about Mars, complete with mobile plants and carnivorous flowers using high-pitched sonic waves to bring down their insect prey!

Now that we have images from the surface of four other worlds in the Solar System—the Moon, Venus, Mars and Titan—such poetic fantasies have faded into prosaic reality. These real extraterrestrial scenes have subconsciously discouraged hopes of finding life on neighboring worlds in the mind of the general public. The Mars Man with his pixy-like features may have seemed possible in a world of migrating plants, but he is seriously out of place on the cratered terrain of the real Martian landscape.

More importantly, advancing knowledge has found the other houses in the Solar System street to be far from welcoming lodgings. Venus is an inferno with a toxic atmosphere that reaches surface pressures similar to those at the bottom of terrestrial oceans. Our barrel-chested Venusian gorilla would be suffocated, crushed and fried to a crisp all within seconds!

Mars may not appear quite as hostile, but its thin air and high flux of solar ultraviolet radiation make it equally lethal for the unprotected inhabitant. As for Jupiter and Saturn . . . they do not even possess true surfaces on which our antenna-sprouting Big Ears could walk. They just keep getting denser and hotter with depth, until their hydrogen atmospheres compress into something like metal!

With accumulating data beamed back from space probes, the picture of Earth that emerged was of an oasis of blue and green in a Solar System that looked ever more hostile with each increase in knowledge. Increasingly, we were being seen to inhabit something which, to borrow the title of a well known science fiction film, could truly be called "this island Earth".

It was becoming apparent that the Earth was not very typical of the planetary members of the Solar System's retinue. Something about it—some singularly unusual set of circumstances—had rendered it especially suitable as a home for life.

One of these unusual circumstances is its distance from the Sun; close enough to ensure temperatures that allow liquid water to exist on the surface, yet not so close as to turn into an oven like Venus.

Distance from the Sun is not the only factor. Far from it, as we shall see later. However, considerations of temperature, and the presence liquid water, have largely been responsible for the concept of 'habitable zones' around stars. These are regions of space where (other things being equal) a planet may possess bodies of liquid water at its surface and may therefore provide a suitable habitat for life (other things, once again, being equal).

Alone of the Sun's primary planets, the Earth inhabits this zone in our own Solar System. Moreover, although there are various estimates as to the zone's width, most astronomers nowadays consider it to be a lot narrower than earlier estimates, most of which had it extending from just outside (or just inside, according to some) the orbit of Venus to beyond the orbit of Mars. With all evidence pointing away from our near neighbors being abodes of life, hope shifted outward from the Solar System to the nearer stars. It was very plausibly argued that if one rather mediocre star (the Sun) could have planets and if even one of these could harbor life, then surely most stars are probably attended by a system of planets and, just as surely, amongst these must be found worlds that look a lot like our own and are populated by beings not too unlike ourselves. The popularity of science fiction 'space operas' such as Star Trek and Star Wars can only be explained in terms of a deep desire that this is really the way things are.

Of course, it was assumed without question that other solar systems would be basically similar to our own. They would be systems of several planets with the largest gas giants ('Jupiter clones') orbiting relatively far from the central star and smaller, rocky, planets ('Earth clones' and 'Venus clones') orbiting closer in. The latter were generally referred to as "terrestrial planets" or more simply "terrestrials". This basically meant planets which are relatively small and posses rocky surfaces, although there may also have been the (perhaps subconscious) implication of their being "Earth-like" in more than a basic physical sense. Science writer and science fiction author Poul Anderson actually subdivided this class into (true) terrestrials—e.g. Earth and Venus—subterrestrials—e.g. Mars, Mercury and the Moon—and superterrestrials or rocky planets larger than Earth. He considered planets in each of these classifications as potential homes for advanced life.[1]

Thus, just as the Earth had formerly been assumed to be a typical planet, so the Solar System was assumed to be typical of planetary systems. This did not imply that all planetary systems would be exact Solar System clones of course. Nor did it preclude the existence of anomalous systems. But it did imply that ours was, at least, a rough approximation of what might be found around other stars.

The discovery of the first exo-planets—in reality, the first exo-solar systems—during the mid 1990s came as just as great a shock as the first close-up images of the Martian surface thirty years earlier; and for much the same reason. Just as Mariner 4 shattered the illusion of a Mars that was in some sense still expected to be like Earth, albeit in an alien way, so the discovery of the first exo-planets shattered the illusion that most planetary systems would somehow look like different versions of our own. Instead, what we found were Jupiter-like planets orbiting so close to their parent stars as to lie within the outer reaches of their coronas (extended atmospheres), other gas giant planets further from their star yet pursuing markedly elliptical orbits and even some cousins of Jupiter sweeping around their sun in orbits so elongated as to appear more representative of those followed by periodic comets than by the planets of our own Solar System.

All of this raises an interesting question; one which few would have dared ask two or three decades ago. Is it possible that Earth and the solar system, of which it is a member, are not really typical after all?

In short, could we be living on an *anomalous* planet in an anomalous solar system?

What About the Copernican Principle?

This question brings us into direct collision with one of the sacred cows of scientific thought, namely, the so-called 'Principle of Mediocrity' (PoM) or Copernican Principle (CoP).

The long held assumption that the Earth is a typical planet orbiting an average star located at a very mediocre place in an ordinary galaxy (that is itself located in a small and unspectacular group of galaxies in a totally unremarkable region of the universe) is, in essence, an interpretation and extension of Copernicus' discovery of the heliocentric nature of the Solar System. The PoM is said to underlie modern science as a sort of philosophical foundation. In essence, it is the assertion that our location in the universe is in no sense special.

If this assertion of mediocrity is correct, it can be argued that the probability of an environment suitable for complex life is quite high. This, in turn, implies that our existence on this particular planet does not imply anything intrinsically unusual about the planet itself, or about its cosmic location.

This latter conclusion may, of course, be challenged even by one who continues to accept the 'mediocrity premise'. Thus, it may be argued, suitable environments may be *necessary* but not *sufficient* for the occurrence of complex life. The question as to whether complex life *must* arise wherever a suitable environment exists has not been answered and we have no compelling reasons to assume that the answer will be in the affirmative. Few who are committed to the mediocrity premise would, however, argue in this way. They would see this line of thought as shifting the burden of special-ness from the planet to the phenomenon of life itself.

The thesis presented here is, however, more radical. We assert that the 'mediocrity premise', that is to say the Copernican Principle itself, is fatally flawed as a *philosophical* principle.

This statement may appear to fly in the face of the last several centuries of scientific discovery. Surely we cannot deny that the Earth is not the centre of the Solar System, that the Solar System is not the centre of the Milky Way and that the Milky Way is not the centre of the universe itself!

No, we cannot deny any of this. Nor do we wish to modify any of it in the least respect.

What we do deny is that we can make the leap of faith (for that is just what it amounts to) and say that, following from the facts outlined above, the Earth must *ipso facto* be typical; that it cannot be in any sense special. In other words, we cannot use the 'Copernican' position of the Earth in space as evidence that Nature somehow has decreed that there is nothing anomalous about the Earth in any manner whatsoever.

But if the Earth really is anomalous—if it is not usual for nature to manufacture planets that are essentially clones of our own—we must ask why it is that we reside on such a cosmic freak. Is this just a fluke or is there some deeper reason behind our place here?

We shall return to this very important question later. First however, let us turn briefly to an issue which, although an aside to our main topic, nevertheless casts an interesting light upon the usual assumption that Copernicus and his early followers were of one mind, philosophically, with those who champion his 'Principle' today.

An important aside

Anyone who reads early scientific literature with an open mind will find—perhaps to his surprise—that the popular account of pre-Copernican cosmology (viz. that prior to Copernicus everybody believed Earth had a special and exalted place in the scheme of things with the rest of the universe revolving about it just a small distance away) has little foundation in pre-Copernican writings themselves. In fact we could argue that Copernicus' discovery of Earth's non-central position in the cosmos has little to say about the principle of mediocrity at all.

Aristotle, from whom the medieval cosmology ultimately descended, certainly differentiated between the 'sublunary' and 'superlunary' realms, but not in such a way as to make the 'sublunary' Earth superior to the 'superlunary' stars. Quite the contrary in fact; the Earth was the place were gross matter accumulated, separating from the superior celestial substance of the superlunary realm. Earth was not seen as being the centre of the universe in the 'good' sense; rather, it was the 'bottom' of the universe. One could really say that for Aristotle, Earth was the universe's sump!

This could be called a 'special' place, but not in any admirable sense. It had the 'special' nature of the cosmic garbage dump!

Likewise Ptolemy, who extended the Aristotelian model of the universe and who was considered the authority on these matters during the late medieval period, certainly cannot be appealed to for support of the supposed 'small' picture of the universe. It is not generally recognized that Ptolemy believed in a universe that was, for all practical considerations, infinite!

Mark his following statements from Chapter Six of the First Book of the *Almagest*, provocatively entitled "*That the Earth Has a Ratio of a Point to the Heavens*";

> Now that the Earth has sensibly the ratio of a point to its distance from the sphere of the so-called fixed stars gets great support from the fact that in all parts of the Earth the sizes and angular distances of the stars at the same times appear everywhere equal and alike. . . . And the Earth is clearly a point also from this fact, that everywhere the planes drawn through the eye, which we call horizons, always exactly cut in half the whole sphere of the heavens.[2]

A geometric point is defined as having position but no magnitude, so by asserting that the Earth is as a point in comparison to the sphere of the fixed stars, Ptolemy is actually asserting that the distance from Earth to the stars is, for all practical purposes, infinite. This is not too different from the assertion of the modern cosmologist and is a far cry from the popular opinion that Ptolemy and his followers believed in a large Earth residing in majesty at the centre of a small, local, universe!

In view of what Aristotle and Ptolemy *really* taught (as against what the post-Copernican revisions of history *say* that they taught), it is not going too far to say that by arguing that Earth is a planet, and therefore similar to the other planets in the superlunary realm, Copernicus actually *elevated* the status of Earth. He lifted it from being the sump of the universe and bestowed upon it the same celestial qualities as the stars themselves. Its distance from the other stars and planets may still have been so great as to make Earth appear as a geometric point by comparison, but at least it was now seen as participating in the same exalted nature as the rest of the universe, 'beyond the Moon'!

This was certainly the opinion of Galileo, who correctly explained the phenomenon popularly known as "the old Moon in the new Moon's arms" (the faintly illuminated disk of the entire Moon as seen during the crescent phase) as Earthshine. He argued that a hypothetical observer on the surface of the Moon would see the Earth as a bright celestial object; something far more dignified than the cosmic sump! Galileo set about to prove this position by presenting arguments

> to demonstrate a very strong reflection of the sun's light from the earth. . . . For I will prove that the earth does have motion, that it surpasses the moon in brightness, and that it is not the *sump where the universe's filth and ephemera collect.*[3] (My emphasis).

Nobody can read these words and continue to maintain that the true Copernicans such as Galileo demoted the role of Earth!

Their opinion of the true place of Earth and humanity was far more in line with the Renaissance humanist revival—and, we might equally say, with the sentiments of Psalm 8; 5-9—than with the Aristotelian viewpoint which saw Earth not just as a point in the immensity of space, but as the point where all the filth of the cosmos was destined to collect. It may be an exaggeration to say that the Copernicans elevated the dignity of man from that of a maggot inhabiting the cosmic garbage dump to a being sharing to a limited degree the rationality of the Creator and inhabiting one of the celestial spheres, but if it is an exaggeration, it is one for which there is support in the writings of the Copernicans themselves!

The Anthropic Principle
Returning to the main thread of our discussion, we may note that much of the purported evidence for the CoP (popularly so termed) is more readily appreciated in terms of what is known as the Anthropic Principle (AP). Very briefly, in its simplest form the AP states that our own existence implies a universe having certain properties, namely those that are compatible with the existence of human life. If the Universe in general, or the Milky Way, the Sun or the Earth in particular, did not have certain features compatible with human life, we would not be here.

In this basic formulation, the AP is simply common sense. It is nothing more or less than the recognition that our existence necessarily implies the presence of certain conditions. No causal connection between our presence and these conditions is implied in this simple version of the Principle. In some of its more extreme forms, the situation becomes much more problematic and the Principle drifts into some strange philosophical ground (thanks mostly to the speculations of philosophical scientists rather than professional philosophers, who tend to be much more conservative these days!). These more fanciful speculations need not concern us however.

Self-evident though the AP may seem, it nevertheless has some far reaching consequences, including many that are generally thought of as being 'Copernican'.

For example, we do not find ourselves at the centre of the Solar System, not because we are somehow 'unworthy' of this high honor, but because conditions there are unsuitable (putting it mildly!) for human life. The Sun is not the place to find intelligent life!

Similarly, the Solar System cannot lie at or near the centre of the Milky Way and remain the home for sentient beings cognizant of that fact. The violent processes taking place at the galactic heartland make life impossible in those regions.

Other anthropic features that make our position in the Universe appear mediocre are more subtle.

For example, we know that life demands the existence of a relatively large abundance of elements heavier than helium. However, because these elements are 'cooked' in the thermonuclear reactions within stars, living organisms (or even the rocky types of planets on which they could live) cannot exist in the vicinity of the ancient stars that formed during the several billion years of cosmic history immediately following the Big Bang. Life, and environments chemically suitable for its existence, is necessarily restricted to those regions of the universe where stars have formed from material that has already been recycled through several generations of stellar interiors. Early stars, arising from the primordial hydrogen and helium synthesized in the Big Bang itself, processed a certain amount of this material into the heavier elements that astronomers rather confusingly call 'metals'. As they explosively ended their lives, these first-generation stars returned some of the heavier elements to the interstellar medium. In this way, the interstellar medium became 'polluted' with traces of 'metals'. The next wave of stars, forming from this slightly 'contaminated' material, necessarily contained traces of the heavy elements that had been denied to the first generation. Nevertheless, the 'metallic content' of these stars was still very meager.

The second generation stars also synthesized 'metals' in their cores and, in time, their largest representatives duly ended their lives violently in Type II supernova explosions, through which material of an even higher 'metal' content was returned to the interstellar medium.

The next wave of stars, therefore, formed from a mixture of interstellar gas and dust containing matter recycled through two previous generations and significantly richer in 'metal' content. Stars formed from this material were similarly metal enriched.

What we have described is, admittedly, an oversimplified picture. It may seem from this that the universe has passed through several discrete waves of star formation and that all regions of the interstellar medium in all galaxies will by now show pretty much the same degree of heavy element enrichment. In actual fact, the real picture is far less tidy and regular. Some galaxies have been unusually active, forming stars at furious rates and passing through the stellar generations rapidly, while others have formed stars only slowly and, even today, remain poor in heavy elements. Recent years have even witnessed the discovery of what appears to be a rather large population of a type of galaxy that escaped detection in earlier times; large, diffuse systems forming comparatively few stars and still mostly comprised of primordial gas. Not surprisingly, these systems remain poor in heavy elements.

Similarly, the dwarf elliptical galaxies which actually make up the lion's share of the galactic population are too lightweight to have retained most of their gaseous component and therefore lost their star-forming ability very early. These diminutive systems consist of small, old and long-lived stars with a low metal content. Their stars are small, because in the stellar world, dwarfs live greatly longer lives than giants and the diminutive stars in these similarly diminutive galaxies continue to shine long after their more massive relatives have faded away or, in some instances, exploded.

Even large galaxies in rich clusters of these systems (especially those toward the central regions of such clusters) tend to show a relatively poor heavy element content when compared with those in small galaxy groups, on the outer fringes of larger clusters, or in the open field. This is due to the higher density of intergalactic material in rich clusters, plus the greatly enhanced probability of frequent collisions between the galaxies themselves. Galactic collisions very seldom bring stars into contact, but they do have the effect of stripping galaxies of their interstellar material, effectively calling a halt to significant new star formation. Even if galaxies within large clusters managed to avoid collision, their continual passage through the gas that fills these systems would probably be enough to strip material from them and severely curtail future star formation.

Within an individual galaxy, the rate of star formation also proceeds at different rates in different regions. Near the centre, where the density of stars and interstellar material is high, star formation rates are naturally higher than those in the sparser outer reaches. In spiral galaxies, such as our own Milky Way, the spectacular spiral arms are also prime regions for vigorous star-forming activity. These arms have been shown to result from the propagation of density waves through the galaxy. Interstellar material is compressed as the wave passes, triggering cascades of star formation.

All of this is reflected in the 'metal' content of stars at differing distances from the galactic heartland. Other things being equal, stars closer to the central regions have the highest 'metal' content while those on the galactic fringes remain 'metal' poor.

In terms of possessing the raw material for both rocky-planet building and life chemistry, the galactic hub would appear at first sight to be the prime cosmic location; however this apparent suitability must be balanced against the violent events taking place there. In fact, the galactic inner city regions are very tough places indeed. Frequent nearby supernova explosions bombard any potentially life bearing world with lethal doses of radiation, and constant nearby passages of stars and molecular clouds disrupt the spheres of comets which probably form a regular feature of any solar system possessing enough water for life to be chemically possible within it. Frequent impacts by comets hurled out of their distant orbits would make conditions perilous for any budding ecosystem on a planet within these solar systems.

G. Gonzalez[4] and other astronomers have put forward the concept of a galactic habitable zone; a rather narrow region surrounding the centre of a galaxy where the stellar neighborhood is sufficiently sparse to avoid frequent comet-cloud disruptions and nearby supernova explosions, yet deep enough within the galaxy to allow rocky planets to form around at least some stars and even permit life chemistry to exist (other things being equal) on the most suitable of these orbs.

There is good evidence that the orbit which the Sun (together with Earth and the rest of the Solar System, of course) pursues around the galactic centre is such that the orbital velocity of the Sun closely matches the speed of propagation of the density wave forming the spiral arms.[5] The special region of the galactic disc where this relationship holds is known as the corotation circle. The distance of this 'circle' from the galactic centre is called the corotation radius.

Although earlier work indicating close proximity of the Solar System's galactic orbit to the corotation circle has been called into question by some astronomers,[6] strong arguments in its support have more recently been advanced by Dias and Lepine.[7] These authors also refer to the issue, already recognized as early as the 1980s,[8,9] that placement of the Solar System close to the corotation circle may be an important requirement for habitability. We know that at present the Sun is located far enough from the dense region of the spiral arms to be safe from comet showers and nearby supernova blasts, but if the two really are essentially in sync, this safe distance will be maintained for a very long time. Thus, the argument runs, a location close to the corotation circle is necessary for the persistence of benign conditions favorable to the long-term maintenance of life. As Dias and Lepine note,

> The proximity of the Sun to the corotation radius means that . . . long periods of time elapse between successive crossings of the spiral arms. . . . Furthermore, the encounters with the spiral arms, with the larger probability of nearby supernova explosions and of gravitational perturbation of the Oort cloud, making more objects like comets to fall toward the inner solar system, could be associated with events of mass extinction of . . . life. . . . Finally, the corotation radius is often considered to be associated with a minimum of star formation. . . . The minimum in the star formation rate close to the Sun is a condition that favors the survival of life on Earth."[10]

If a move away from the corotation circle would inevitably result in an increase in the frequency of life-inhibiting events such as nearby supernovas and comet impacts, even a slight change in the Sun's galactic orbit would eventually spell disaster for terrestrial life. Life-endangering events have certainly occurred during the history of planet Earth, but thanks to our proximity to the corotation circle, they occur very infrequently, allowing terrestrial life to recover from the trauma. Outside this narrow circle, the time between catastrophic events may not be sufficient for life's recovery.

All in all, the galactic habitable zone is quite narrow and effectively fixes the Solar System's position to a small region within the Milky Way galaxy.

The Sun's orbit around the centre of the Milky Way also seems to be peculiar—indeed, anomalous—in so far as it remains oddly close to the galactic plane. Over the vast stretches of cosmic time that have elapsed since the Milky Way's formation, mutual gravitational perturbations of the stars and clouds of interstellar material that comprise it has tended to 'pump up' the orbits of these objects and cause them to progressively stray from the mean plane of the galaxy. Generally speaking, the older the object, the more time it has had for any variations in its orbit to be enlarged. Older objects will normally be expected to stray further from the galactic plane than younger ones. In the main, this is just what is found. Very young objects such as giant molecular clouds and the brilliant but short-lived O and B type stars are found very close to the plane, typically straying no more than 150-300 light years from it. Conversely, solar type stars of around the Sun's age mostly stray from between 600 and 1,100 light years from mid plane. Curiously however, the Sun remains within 250 light years of the galactic mid plane, more characteristic of objects one thousandth of its age.

This position close to the mid plane is probably significant in shielding us from exposure to too much cosmic radiation from the violent events of the galactic heartland. It is fortunate indeed that we are afforded this position within the Galaxy, while yet possessing enough heavy elements to enable terrestrial planets to form.

Young Sun-like stars existing similarly close to the mid-plane are likely to be even richer in heavy elements, but that is not necessarily a good thing for habitability. A 'metal' content significantly higher than solar probably means a thicker pre-planetary disc which in turn could imply a greater propensity for giant planets to migrate inward. It is probably no coincidence that there appears to be a correlation between high 'metal' content and the propensity for a system to possess 'hot jupiters' that have presumably migrated inward from more remote regions of the pre-planetary nebula. Such a migrating planet would not bode well for any nascent terrestrial globes that might be present within the potentially habitable zone of one of these systems. Also, high 'metal' content would presumably imply the existence of more comets and asteroids in a system and therefore a higher impact rate on any terrestrial planets that may have managed to survive.

The relative proportions of the different heavy elements in the interstellar medium probably change with time. Thus, as the numbers of Type II supernova dwindle over the age of the Galaxy, radioactive elements become scarcer. This probably means that potential Earth clones formed during the last few millions of years do not possess quantities of radioactive elements sufficient to drive plate tectonics beyond the planet's youth. Given the importance to life of terrestrial plate tectonics (about which more will be said later), these worlds are likely to end up looking more Venusian than Terrestrial, even if they are located right in the middle of a circumstellar habitable zone.[11]

A consideration of the points raised by the above discussion once again reveals that what at first sight may appear as 'Copernican mediocrity' is actually anthropic-determined selection. The Sun's position away from the galactic centre has already been commented upon, but we may now understand that it is also important that the home galaxy itself is a member of a small and seemingly 'unimportant' galaxy cluster. If our 'Local Group' (as astronomers call our home cluster) was a large grouping of hundreds or thousands of galaxies, chances are that the Milky Way would have been stripped of star forming material long before Earth was formed. This would have been even more likely had our galaxy occupied a central position in one of the larger galactic groupings.

Anthropic considerations, however, determine that we are not at the very fringes of the galaxy (due to lack of sufficient concentration of 'metals' there) and they also place a somewhat anti-Copernican restriction on the size of our home galaxy. It cannot be too small and seemingly insignificant, as its population of stars would then be too small for the synthesis of enough 'metals' at the time of the Solar System's formation. The Sun may still have formed, but it would probably have been without its familiar retinue of planets. Actually, anthropic considerations decree that our galaxy must be a heavyweight; amongst the largest 5% in the universe in fact!

Yet, these same considerations militate against our existence in one of the *very* largest galaxies. These are mostly giant ellipticals believed to have formed by the merging of two major spiral galaxies similar to our own. The problem with these is that the merger also stripped them of most of their star-forming material and the orbits of their stars have been deflected into very elongated orbits which take them close to the dangerous galactic heartland.

In short, anthropic considerations do not always mimic 'Copernican' predictions, but they reproduce them sufficiently often to give the illusion that there is some underlying principle of nature that keeps us in a lowly place.

Anthropic considerations explain our position away from the centre of the Solar System and the Solar System's position away from the galactic centre. They explain why our galaxy is a member of a small group rather than of a large cluster. They also explain why we inhabit a relatively small planet instead of one that dominates its solar system in the manner of, say, Jupiter. These planets necessarily possess atmospheres that are vast, dense, and poisonous, to say nothing of a gravitational pull that would crush any conceivable macro-organism, with the highly unlikely exception of fanciful living gas-bags suspended in their atmospheres!

On the other hand, anthropic considerations do not allow very small planets such as Mercury, Mars or the Moon to be inhabited by beings like us. One of the problems faced by these diminutive worlds is that if they are situated within the potential habitable zone of their solar system, they receive too much energy from their star to enable retention of a dense atmosphere. Moreover, they lack sufficient magnetic field to shield their surfaces against the energetic particles of the so-called Solar Wind.

We have already noted how space research has highlighted the unusual nature of Earth. Our home planet stands out from the rest of the Sun's retinue as an oasis of life in a hostile solar system. This was not what the early 'Copernicans' expected. Neither was the far more recent discovery that every other solar system is not simply a copy of our own. Indeed, of the solar systems thus far discovered, none looks much like ours at all. Not only that, but they differ from ours in ways that make them appear less likely to harbor a planet where life may flourish. The shock that a previous generation of astronomers encountered upon finding the real nature of our neighboring planets is being repeated by the present generation as the real nature of other planetary systems is uncovered, although it is still too early to gain any true picture as to how our own system compares with the majority. The sample is still quite small and the methods of discovery bias the statistics toward systems that differ from our own. Solar systems having large planets close to their parent stars are more readily discovered because the gravitational tug from a nearby giant planet orbiting rapidly at small distance is more quickly apparent to astronomers than the slow displacement caused by something at Jupiter-like distances from its sun. Nevertheless, during the coming years the number of stars which have been observed long enough for these more sedate wobbles to become apparent will increase, giving us a better assessment of how common solar systems at least relatively similar to our own may be.

The fact remains however that systems like our own, that is to say, those which allow for the existence of a life-friendly planet, are far from being the only ones in the galaxy.

The Perfect Cosmological Principle
Early last century, Albert Einstein put forward an assumption that the universe will look essentially the same in which ever direction we look; more technically, that the universe is homogeneous and isotropic on very large scales. He put this forward as a working assumption—albeit a very plausible one—rather than a deep metaphysical insight into the nature of the universe. It was not based upon a 'Copernican' premise; however it has since assumed this association and its truth largely taken as a given fact about the cosmos. In its 'Copernican' formulation, the 'Cosmological Principle' (CP) underlies most cosmological speculation today.

However, if it is correct as a basic philosophical principle of nature, one would expect it to hold not just in the three dimensions of space, but also in the four-dimensional space-time manifold. Surely this must follow logically from Einstein's Theory of General Relativity in which time is included as a fourth dimension of space (or, more accurately, of the space-time continuum). But if time can be treated as another dimension of the same manifold that includes the three familiar spatial dimensions, *and* if the CP holds in the three dimensions, it logically follows that it must equally hold in the fourth (time) dimension.

In other words, if the CP is as basic to the nature of Reality as its supporters suppose, it must exclude the possibility of special moments in time on the same basis and for the same reason as it excludes special places in space. If Einstein is correct, there is no intrinsic difference between an instant in time and a point in space. They are both locations in a four-dimensional manifold.

In the early 1950s, this line of thinking led three Cambridge scientists—Fred Hoyle, Herman Bondi and Thomas Gold—to put forward a four-dimensional advance on the CP; the Perfect Cosmological Principle or PCP. The logic of this move was impeccable. In fact, we argue that if the CP is correct, the PCP must logically and inevitably follow in a universe describable by the equations of Einstein. Conversely, if the PCP is found to be incorrect, the CP must fall with it. The implications of logic operate in both directions. Any predictions following from the PCP will, therefore, also act as tests for the validity of the CP.

The most important prediction of the PCP was the Steady State (SS) cosmology. This follows inevitably from the PCP in that the latter necessarily precludes the occurrence of a Big Bang creation event. The moment $T = 0$ as postulated by the Big Bang theorists is precisely the kind of special moment in time that the PCP excludes. Indeed, it was the philosophical force of the PCP which these scientists saw as the major attraction of SS cosmology. It seemed to them to be the logical and inevitable conclusion of the CP. Moreover, as the CP had long been conflated with the CoP, the SS came to be viewed as another victory in the ongoing Copernican Revolution.

We wholeheartedly agree with their logic. The only problem is, increasing observational evidence has consistently supported the Big Bang cosmology at the expense of the SS!

Very few cosmologists these days place any faith in the PCP, although some have publicly bemoaned the passing of the SS on the grounds that the loss of the PCP represented a blow to the beauty of the universe.

But why was the PCP thought to be especially "beautiful"?

It appeared to be beautiful, precisely because it presented us with the ultimate Copernican vision of the universe. As such, its verification would have provided a powerful argument in favour of the CoP.

It appears strange, not to say illogical, that the CoP/PoM/CP survived unscathed following the fall of the PCP. Retaining this principle, whilst rejecting the PCP, is a little like rejecting the existence of atoms whilst retaining the standard explanation for chemical reactions; an explanation which itself rests upon the validity of atomic theory!

Of course, it does not automatically follow that because there is a unique moment in time ($T = 0$) or because there is clear evidence of cosmic evolution over time (i.e. the universe appeared very different in the distant past), that there *must* be special places or that the universe will appear radically different when observed from different regions, but it does leave that possibility logically open. In other words, somebody postulating special places or special regions cannot be dismissed out of hand as talking nonsense or of violating a basic philosophical principle of nature. The question will be settled, if it is settled at all, on the basis of observational evidence, not by appealing to allegedly *a priori* principles.

Thus, if we suppose that some phenomenon, X, was discovered at just one location in the universe, it would not be violating any fundamental principle of nature to assert that X occurred nowhere else. Just as we do not violate any basic principle by asserting the existence of one Big Bang at one moment of time, so we are not in violation of any basic principle if we assert that X is unique to one particular spatial location. We may be incorrect in our assertion, but that is a matter for observation, not of *a priori* deduction. It may be that X has appeared at one place and will spread eventually throughout the observable cosmos, or X may persist indefinitely at its place of origin without spreading any further, or yet again, X may persist for a time at its place of origin and then disappear, never again to reoccur. Asserting any of these possibilities does not violate any fundamental principle of nature.

We should also add that if X occurs under, and only under, conditions Y, there is no *a priori* certainty that it will occur in another place where Y is repeated. This would only be true if Y was both necessary *and sufficient* for the existence of X. But that is something that we cannot automatically assume. It is equally possible that Y will be the necessary, but not the sufficient, condition for the occurrence of X; that although the conditions that we have designated as Y are essential for the existence of X, these conditions alone require something further—something over and above the set of conditions themselves—for X to occur. As a very simple and homely example, consider an incandescent bulb connected to a source of electricity by a system of switch and wires. The connection of wires, power source and switch is a necessary condition for the lamp to give light, but it may be connected without actually lighting up. What is needed is for someone to decide to throw the switch. The connections of wires etc. are indeed necessary, but they are less than sufficient. The lamp will not work unless and until somebody turns the switch on!

Our 'Special' Planet

"Special" may be a word holding emotive connotations considered undesirable by some readers. It is, we admit, a loaded word in so far as it tends to imply a degree of approval. We say something is "special" when we wish, not merely to imply that it is different in a unique (or at least highly unusual) manner, but also that its characteristic difference makes it somehow 'better' than other basically similar things.

Now, Earth may indeed appear to us to be different from (say) Mars or Venus in a highly beneficial way. It harbors conditions which permit our existence, in contrast to those neighboring worlds which we may characterize (in a sense almost disparagingly) as being "barren" or "desolate". From our point of view, Earth possesses a value that Venus and Mars do not. We may deny in principle that one planet has an intrinsic worth that is lacking in another, but that does not necessarily determine the way we think in practice. Suppose, for instance, that astronomers discovered three comets heading straight for Venus, Mars and Earth and further suppose that we had the technological ability to deflect just one of them. Would there be any debate as to which would be deflected?

This sense of "being special" however, does not say anything about the intrinsic "special-ness" of our planet. We find our houses special, even though they may look exactly like the neighbors' and millions of other houses in our city. They are special to us, but not intrinsically so. In the same way, Earth would be special from our point of view irrespective of whether it is one of a kind or whether there are billions of similar worlds scattered throughout the universe.

Our question though, is whether the Earth is "different" in a more fundamental sense. Perhaps we should avoid the loaded word "special" in this context and instead substitute the more neutral "anomalous". Our question then breaks down into whether the Earth is anomalous and, if it is, whether its anomalous nature plays an important role in determining its habitability. If it is anomalous, and if its anomalous nature can be shown to be a necessary (though not necessarily a *sufficient*) condition for the existence of life, then we may indeed declare that the Earth is not simply anomalous but truly special in a real and objective sense.

Even our earlier cursory look at our home planet's position in the cosmic environment has revealed that we are prime astronomical real estate. To this degree we may already declare Earth to be at least somewhat anomalous. It is, we might say, "environmentally anomalous" and therefore likely to be a *relatively* unlikely occurrence on these grounds alone.

But does Earth also possess intrinsically anomalous features?

Does our home planet possess features that would make it anomalous irrespective of its location in the cosmic environment?

A peculiar planet!

In this large and complex universe, one thing that we can be sure to find is variety! The more complex an object, the more features it will possess and the less likely it becomes that it has an exact twin. Two stars of exactly the same type may appear essentially indistinguishable, but that is because stars are relatively simply objects. Jovian planets are also relatively simple in so far as they too are basically balls of gas compressed by their own gravity. But terrestrial worlds show a more complex face. The solid surfaces of these smaller planets record a complex history. Meteorite impacts scared them with craters, while volcanic eruptions and crustal movements sculptured their own characteristic features.

Terrestrial worlds possessing significant atmospheres reveal the further effects of erosion. Rocky planets wear their past on their faces; they have been sculptured by the hands of Time and History as, indeed, have we. My life's experiences and the subtle forces that have shaped the history of my family and helped influence my genes will not be the same as yours. There have simply been too many different factors in operation, too great a complexity of converging influences to make it mathematically probable that an exactly similar constellation of factors will occur in the personal history of another human being. I am unique; but so are you. So is each person who has ever walked on this planet; or who ever will.

Likewise, each planet has been the recipient of so many influences that the chance of its exact repetition within the observable universe is infinitesimal. Just as you are unique and I am unique, so Earth is unique. But then, so is Mars and so is Venus. . . .

Uniqueness in this sense does not necessarily imply anomaly. Each person is unique, though each person is not anomalous. However, part of some people's uniqueness does constitute an anomaly. The outstanding genius is surely an anomaly in having an IQ conspicuously greater than the vast majority of people. It is possible that somebody could be so anomalous as to be literally one of a kind; a person whose uniqueness is obvious to all (for instance, somebody with an IQ well beyond anything seen in any other person or somebody who, like Lazarus Long in Robert Heinlen's novels, had a genetic anomaly that rendered him physically immortal).

Our question about Planet Earth effectively asks whether it possesses some equivalent anomaly. Is it obviously different from other planets of the same general type? Does something set it apart as a true rarity—even a 'one-off'—in the way that Lazarus Long's genetic 'problem' set him apart from the rest of the human race?

We do not need to search long before finding some ways in which our home planet differs from the other rocky or 'terrestrial' worlds in the Solar System. (Incidentally, I am using the word "terrestrial" to mean any planet that is rocky, rather than icy, and larger than asteroidal size. This is the normal use of the term, as distinct from Poul Anderson's more restrictive meaning mentioned earlier).

One difference is immediately noted. Earth is the only Solar System terrestrial planet which possesses a moon having a diameter comparable with that of the primary. Although the Moon is smaller than the Earth, the difference in diameters between primary and satellite is nowhere near as great as that between Mars and its moons. The Earth/Moon duet could almost be called a double planet.

Another important difference is the continuing process of plate tectonics that slowly but constantly reshapes the surface of our world. This is the process that raised the continents and folded the mountain ranges of Earth; two geological features that also differentiate our world from its neighbors. The raised areas of Venus appear to be similar to the continental regions of Earth, so that planet probably possessed similar plate tectonic activity long ago, but its 'plate tectonic engine' seized up when the planet was still quite young.

Compared to its neighbors, Mars and Venus, Earth has a very thin crust. Sometimes this is stated with an almost Doomsday inflection in the voice, as if to draw attention to the fact that a solid protective sheath thinner (in comparison to the planet's diameter) than the shell of an egg is all that separates us from the scorching planetary interior. However, it is precisely this crustal thinness that enables plate tectonics to continue into the present epoch. We shall see in a little while that this is an important benefit, not a detriment, to life on this planet.

Our planet also possesses the unusual feature of a global magnetic field. Gas giants, such as Jupiter, possess strong planetary magnetic fields, but (if the Solar System's terrestrial planets are representative of the class as a whole) the smaller objects appear to be mostly devoid of significant fields; at least, ones that persist for times comparable to the age of the Solar System. Mercury has a very weak field, and Martian rocks yield evidence of a more magnetic earlier age, but Earth is the only Solar System terrestrial planet that possesses a field of any appreciable strength today.

This is just as well for us, because the magnetic field acts as a shield against those high energy particles that constantly boil off the Sun and sweep through interplanetary space as a "solar wind" of plasma. Without our magnetic shield, we would not only experience dangerously enhanced levels of radiation at surface level, but the upper atmosphere of Earth would steadily erode away through the action of this "wind".

In particular, unprotected exposure to the Solar wind would have a desiccating effect upon our planet. Molecules of water vapor would be dissociated into their components of oxygen and hydrogen. The former would quickly combine with other elements to form oxides, while hydrogen, too light for retention by the gravitational attraction of a planet as small as Earth, would be lost to space.

Amongst the terrestrial planets of the Solar System, Earth stands out as being the only world with quantities of liquid water at its surface. If an extraterrestrial were to visit our Solar System, this is probably the most striking feature that he (she? it??) would notice. Earth is strikingly different from its neighboring planets by having all three states of water—solid, liquid and gas—evident at its surface. It is not alone in possessing water per se (Mars has water ice, although the amount is controversial at the time of writing) and there may have been liquid water on the surfaces of both Mars and Venus for a geologically brief period during the youth of the Solar System, but none of the other terrestrial worlds possesses liquid surface water today. Conditions on these worlds do not permit it. Even on Mars, the most benign of our neighbors, liquid water would boil away immediately upon exposure to the low atmospheric pressure at its surface.

Indeed, we could go a step further and note that ours is the only Solar System terrestrial planet possessing surface conditions that enable the three states of *matter* to exist at its surface. Indeed, if we were to consider all the solid bodies in the Solar System, the only other world to rival Earth in this respect is the Saturnian moon Titan. As an icy object however, this giant moon does not rate as a true terrestrial world according to the criteria being used here. The three states of matter are, apparently, possible on Titan as there is clear evidence that this moon's surface has been eroded by the action of liquid methane, although the question remains open as to whether there are any permanent bodies of this liquid there or whether it is only present as transitory ponds and occasional streams.

However, water plays two important roles on Earth that methane does not play on Titan.

First of all, it is a necessary solvent for life, so its abundance on our planet is an important factor making life possible here. Too much water, on the other hand, may work against the presence of life. A complete water world—one without continents and possessing, at most, temporary volcanic islands—may not be habitable due to too great a dilution of nutrients in its global ocean. Moreover, a planet without dry land would not be capable of providing suitable habitats for intelligent and, especially, *technological* life. A fine balance of continental land and ocean may well be a requirement for complex life; or even for the existence of life at all.

Secondly, abundant water is needed to act as a lubricant for sustained plate tectonic activity. Without a sufficient store of water, Earth's plate tectonic engine would seize, internal heat (no longer expended in the work of crustal plate movement) would build up and eventually burst forth in periodic bouts of intense global volcanism.

Plate tectonics makes the carbon cycle possible. This too is essential to Earth's habitability by regulating the exchange of carbon-containing molecules between ocean, air and land. Photosynthesis by land plants and phytoplankton near the surface of the oceans draws carbon dioxide from the atmosphere and uses this in the synthesis of organic matter. Zooplankton then consumes much of this organic material close to the sunlit ocean surface. In time, these organisms die and their carbonate and silicate skeletons drift downward through the ocean depths, eventually settling onto the ocean floor. Finally, the accumulated carbonate and silicate material is pulled down into the Earth as the continental shelves subduct.

Meanwhile above the ocean surface, rainwater made mildly acidic by dissolved atmospheric carbon dioxide reacts with minerals in exposed surface rocks. Rivers and streams carry these dissolved silica dioxide, calcium and bicarbonate ions down into the oceans where they are removed by phytoplankton and zooplankton and, to a lesser extent, by shellfish and corals, and incorporated into their skeletons. Eventually deposited onto the ocean floor, these are subsequently subducted and pressure-cooked deep within the Earth's crust and the carbon dioxide released back into the atmosphere through volcanoes and springs. It is this carbon cycle that prevents carbon dioxide from building up into dangerously high levels in the atmosphere or, conversely, from being removed from the air altogether. In this way, the planet avoids a runaway greenhouse on the one hand and a serious fall in global temperatures (with the danger of runaway glaciation) on the other. The carbon cycle has rightly been termed the planet's thermostat.

It may seem strange to be drawing attention to this next feature, but we should also add that ours is the only Solar System body from which 'perfect' solar eclipses may be observed.

What do we mean by a 'perfect' eclipse?

The term was coined by Professor Guillermo Gonzalez[12] to refer to a total solar eclipse in which an eclipsing body, for example, the Moon barely covers the Sun's brilliantly glowing photosphere or 'surface'. Such an eclipse lasts long enough for observations to be made and for the full grandeur of the event to be appreciated. The apparent diameter of the obscuring Moon is just large enough to blot out the photosphere yet not so large as to obscure the colorful chromosphere and flame-like prominence around the solar rim.

At first sight, this property of our home planet might seem to be nothing more than an interesting anomaly, albeit a welcome one for those of its inhabitants fortunate enough to witness such a spectacular phenomenon. But a closer look reveals something much more interesting.

'Perfect' solar eclipses could not occur except for a coincidence that is almost incredible. We are speaking, of course, of the remarkable match in the apparent diameters of the Sun and Moon as observed from the surface of the Earth.

We are so accustomed to this that most of us seldom give it a second thought. Many elementary books on astronomy mention the coincidence, only to dismiss it with a wave of the metaphorical hand. Nevertheless, if we reflect on this for a few moments, we cannot help but be impressed by its occurrence. We may even be led to wonder if there is some underlying, subtle, factor operating here.

There is no real physical reason for imagining that the apparent, angular, size—that is to say, the arc that they subtend as seen in the sky—of two such diverse objects should be even approximately similar. Hypothetical observers on the surfaces of the other planets in the Solar System would notice a major dissimilarity between the apparent dimensions of the Sun as it appears in *their* skies and the apparent size of *their* moons. Curiously however, our Moon has a true diameter of approximately 1/400 that of the Sun, yet its distance from us is also approximately 1/400 the solar distance.

If we are to seek possible reasons for this coincidence, we must first inquire as to why the Sun and Moon have the apparent diameters that we see.

The apparent diameter of the Sun, as viewed from the Earth, is actually quite strictly determined to within narrow limits. At least, it is so determined if we are going to be here to appreciate it!

Thus, if the Sun appeared in our skies significantly larger than it does it would need to be either (a) closer or (b) intrinsically larger.

In the latter instance, even a slight increase in the diameter of a star means a significant increase in its heat output, so only a slightly larger Sun would result in a critical increase in terrestrial temperature. But even if the Sun was merely *apparently* larger—even if the same Sun that now lights our days was just a little nearer Earth—the extra heat would suffice to trigger climatic catastrophe. Probably a decrease in the radius of Earth's orbit by as little as two percent would be sufficient to trigger a global runaway greenhouse effect that would leave out planet looking more like Venus than the Earth we know!

The opposite is true for a smaller apparent solar diameter. Either an intrinsically smaller Sun or a more distant one would mean less heat received by our home planet. Opinions differ as to how much cooler our world could become before runaway glaciation set in, but it is likely that the margin is quite narrow, unless larger quantities of greenhouse gases (principally carbon dioxide) were introduced into the atmosphere. This would, however, create problems for large oxygen-breathing land mammals, including humans, whose survival requires low atmospheric concentrations of this gas.

The question as to how much our distance from the Sun could be increased without catastrophe is complicated by the fact that the Sun was fainter and cooler in the distant past. The balance between maintaining an early greenhouse effect sufficient to keep the Earth from freezing solid while enabling it to fall short of boiling in more recent ages is one of the foremost examples of a fine-tuning balancing act. But this balancing act would probably have been toppled had the Earth been only a little further from the Sun in those remote times. Life on this planet might be able to survive (though not necessarily happily) a certain degree of global cooling today, but there is reason to think that we came near to permanent disaster level some 2.3 billion years ago during the great Snowball Earth period, when the Sun was only 85% as bright as it is today. A slight shift outward in the Earth's orbit may have had more devastating effects then than now. Indeed, the effects may have been so devastating that terrestrial life might not have recovered. At least, that would appear to be an implication of the explanation of the Snowball put forward by J. Kirschvink and R. Kopp et al. in 2005.[13]

According to Kirschvink and his team, the atmosphere of Earth was, for a long time prior to 2.3 billion years ago, rich in methane. This is a greenhouse gas dozens of times more efficient than carbon dioxide. These authors argue that it was due to the relative abundance of this gas that global temperatures prior to the Snowball period were similar to those of today, despite the faintness of the early Sun. This implies that, had this greenhouse gas not been removed from the atmosphere, the planet would have cooked as the Sun's light and heat output increased. According to these authors, the most likely removal agent appears to have been oxygen. But where did this gas originate on the early Earth?

Life existed on Earth way back then, but it was mostly in the form of bacteria that depended for their metabolism upon sulfides and iron. But about 2.3 billion years ago, Kirschvink and colleagues argue, there appeared on Earth a new type of bacteria—cyanobacteria—possessing the ability to break down water and release oxygen into the atmosphere. In another of those improbable 'coincidences' that keep raising their head when life on Earth is discussed, about this same time, Earth entered a period of cooler temperatures and increased glaciation. Glaciers ground away a great deal of continental rock and carried this down into the oceans, providing the small populations of oxygen-producing bacteria with a feast of nutrients. Stimulated by this their numbers multiplied rapidly throughout the primitive oceans. Oxygen began to pour into the atmosphere, removing methane and eliminating the greenhouse effect.

For tens of millions of years, the Earth froze. There is debate about just how deep the freeze became, but many experts think that even the equatorial oceans were covered by ice over a kilometer thick throughout this period. Average global temperatures fell to -50 C; even lower at the poles.

Most life died, but some micro-organisms managed to survive by breathing the new gas—oxygen—that by then had come to constitute a large part of the atmosphere. The waste product of this oxygen breathing was carbon dioxide, and over tens of millions of years the slow accumulation of this gas in the atmosphere brought about a new greenhouse situation in which the Earth again warmed and the great ice sheets melted. This new greenhouse was not as effective as the methane one tens of millions of years earlier, but it did not need to be. The Sun had brightened in the meantime and Earth was therefore receiving more solar warmth than it had been prior to the great freeze.

During the Snowball period, temperatures at the poles may have fallen well below -50 C. Had they gone down as far as -78.5 C, carbon dioxide itself would have frozen into dry ice and been removed from the atmosphere. Had this happened, the second (CO2-driven) greenhouse may not have occurred and the planet may never have pulled out of the Snowball, in spite of the warming Sun. If Earth had formed just a little farther from the Sun, it may have remained a frozen world to this day. (Incidentally, had its velocity of rotation been greater the temperature gradient between equator and poles would have been enhanced and the polar temperatures may have reached the freezing point of carbon dioxide, even at our present solar distance; but that is another story, as we shall very shortly see!). In short, the apparent size of the Sun as seen from Earth is fixed within narrow limits, not because of any physical necessity but because any appreciable alteration would make conditions on this planet intolerable for human observers! The nature and distance of the Sun forms part of what we might call the 'constellation of factors' determining our home planet's habitable potential.

Is there a similar anthropic clue in the Moon's apparent size?

On the face of it, the angular diameter of the Moon must seem totally irrelevant to Earth's habitability. Yet, superficial appearances can be deceptive.

The Moon certainly does play some role in terrestrial conditions. Think of the tides, for instance. Without a large satellite, the only tides occurring would be those raised by the Sun, amounting to a range of about one third of the actual tidal variation.

Tides wash nutrients from the land and mix them with the oceans, creating a fertile inter-tidal zone where the land is regularly immersed in ocean waters and where large populations of inter-tidal organisms can flourish. Recent research has also shown that tides exercise a hitherto unknown effect on the deep ocean. Contrary to what had long been believed, it turns out that as much as one third of all the lunar tidal energy is expended along the rugged regions of the deep ocean floor. This suggests that it may be one of the major forces driving ocean currents. Furthermore, because ocean currents play an important role in regulating terrestrial climate, it seems that tides may have further reaching consequences than anyone had hitherto imagined.

Be that as it may, even the most basic function of tides—namely, the mixing of nutrients—is of major importance to the balance of life in our oceans, and without the lunar tides, these would almost certainly have been biologically far poorer regions. This, in turn, would have had important, and probably dire, consequences for land-based life.

Needless to say, an intrinsically smaller or more remote Moon would have resulted in weaker tides; a very small and/or very remote satellite being little different in practice to no Moon at all.

On the other hand, a more massive or closer Moon would have given rise to larger tidal effects. Erosion caused by tides would then have been greater and, unless plate tectonic activity had been correspondingly greater (with a higher incidence of earthquakes as an inevitable consequence!) erosion of the continental landmasses would long ago have turned our planet into a water world.

Another problem with a larger and/or closer Moon would be slower rotation of the Earth and a consequent increase in the length of day. This would not be good news for moderate temperatures. For instance, if summer temperatures in a hot region become almost unbearable by 3PM after, say, 10 hours of sunlight, imagine how 12 'midnight' would feel following 19 hours of daylight!

Moreover, a decrease in the rotation rate leads to a decrease in the temperature gradient between equator and poles. Slowly rotating worlds as different as Venus and Titan show very little difference in temperature between their equatorial and polar regions. A slowly rotating Earth would have similarly even temperatures across the entire spectrum of latitudes.

Even more serious would be the probable loss of a global magnetic field which, as we have seen, offers our best protection from the deleterious effects of the Solar Wind.

In the most extreme case, the Earth's rotation and the Moon's orbit could become locked, such that our day equaled the lunar month.

A very large or very close Moon would probably induce such powerful tidal effects within the Earth's crust as to turn the entire planet into a violent lava spurting Tartarus. No need to concern ourselves with ocean tides in that situation. The oceans would have boiled away!

We conclude, therefore, that a substantially larger or smaller Moon would render conditions on this planet a lot less favorable for the existence of complex life. Nevertheless, the above considerations continue to allow a moderate range in lunar diameters. A *significantly* larger or smaller Moon may be ruled out, but a *slightly* larger or smaller one remains possible on these considerations alone. Are there, perhaps, other factors that restrain the Moon's diameter so severely that virtually *any* change involves serious anthropic consequences?

Such factors may indeed exist!

During the past couple of decades, several people have pointed to a stabilizing effect exercised by the Moon on the precession (basically, the 'axis wobble') of the Earth. The emerging picture is one of a potentially gyrating Earth held in check only by the stabilizing presence of an oversized satellite companion. Without the Moon's presence, Earth's axis would swing wildly through tens of degrees over geologically brief periods of time, creating ecological havoc and possibly rendering complex land-based life impossible.

This thesis was developed further by British geologist, Dave Waltham, in a paper published in 2004.[14] Some eleven years earlier, J Laskar and colleagues also addressed the issue of the Moon's effect on Earth's axial stability. These researchers discovered a potential resonance existing between the precession rate of the Earth and any potential gravitational perturbations from one of the other major planets.[15] Specifically, they found that chaotic variations in the obliquity of Earth's axis would occur if its precession rate approximated the nodal precession rate of another major planet. In fact, the largest nodal precession is that of Saturn (that is to say, the points—nodes—at which the orbit of this planet crosses the plane of the Solar System shift more rapidly than those of the other planets). Nevertheless, the rate of this shift is little more than half that of the shift in Earth's obliquity, so in actual fact the potential for chaos is not realized and the obliquity of Earth's axis remains relatively constant.

Waltham investigated how this might change if the mass of the Moon was varied. If he is correct in his findings, it would seem that Earth is a lot closer to chaos than anybody had ever realized!

Waltham found that an increase of a mere 2% in the Moon's mass would bring the Earth's axial precession rate into resonance with the gravitational perturbations of Saturn. Had our Moon been only 2% more massive, Earth's axis would go through obliquity variations exceeding 50 degrees over periods of a few millions of years. Interestingly, Waltham remarked that a mass increase of the required order would add just 22 kilometers to the Moon's diameter. As viewed from Earth, this increase would pass unnoticed by casual observers.

Waltham also found that the rotational velocity of Earth would plunge, and the length of our days skyrocket, if the Moon's mass was increased by a very modest amount. A mass gain of only around 1% would significantly increase the length of day.

Conversely, a decrease of similar magnitude in the Moon's mass causes the Earth's rotation to significantly speed up and the day to drastically shorten. This would have the effect of increasing temperature differences between equator and pole, presumably wreaking havoc with the delicate climatic balance. The effects of this on land based life have not been worked out in detail, but they could hardly be good. Indeed, recalling our earlier remarks about the 'Snowball' period of Earth's history, polar temperatures on a faster spinning Earth may then have reached the freezing point of carbon dioxide. As we have already remarked, this may have prevented an eventual greenhouse warming by removing this gas from the atmosphere!

If Waltham is correct, it seems that the apparent size of the Moon as seen from Earth's surface is at least as tightly constrained as that of the Sun and that the occurrence of 'perfect' solar eclipses is nothing short of an anthropic necessity!

There is a good deal more to be said about solar eclipses, and we shall return to the subject in a later chapter. Enough has been said however, to show that even an apparent 'mere coincidence' can signify the presence of surprisingly profound factors impinging on the issue of our planet's habitability.

A surprising number of these anomalies are thought to stem from a catastrophic event that took place as the Earth was forming. Before any life existed on our world, during the era when the planets were still building, proto-Earth sustained the biggest blow that it has ever experienced. It was struck by a planetary body that may have been larger than Mars!

The colliding body struck proto-Earth at a shallow, glancing, angle, effectively peeling off much of the latter's crust and blasting its developing atmosphere into space. The impacting body disintegrated, much of its outer layers mixing with the crust that had been blasted off proto-Earth to form a ring of rocky material close to the planet. The impacting object's iron core, it is thought, fell to Earth and sunk through the ocean of magma into which the impact had converted the surface of the planet, finally mingling with the planet's original metallic core.

It is probable that proto-Earth rotated a lot less rapidly than the present day Earth, but the impact would have greatly increased its rotational velocity. Immediately following the event, it rotated significantly faster than it does today.

From this singular event, the Earth was left with a thinner crust and a larger metallic core than it 'should have' possessed. One result of this was our anomalous persisting plate tectonic activity. Also, the extra material deposited in Earth's core probably made a significant contribution to the strength and persistence of the global magnetic field.

The stripping away of Earth's primordial atmosphere was probably an important factor in preventing the accumulation of a dense shroud like the gaseous mantel that literally chokes the life out of Venus. Bereft of air following the great impact, the young Earth accumulated a new and less dense envelope through volcanism and the impact of volatile-bearing meteorites from the outer asteroid belt, together with a smaller contribution from comets and their debris.

The time of impact, angle of impact and even the direction from which the impacting object hit all appear to have played critical roles in the resulting development of our planet. The Earth needed to be at a particular stage of development for the story to have turned out well for the subsequent development of terrestrial life. Too early or too late, and the effects would have been different.

Had the trajectory of the impacting object been too steep, the Earth may have been smashed to pieces. Maybe the debris from proto-Earth and impacting object would have re-accreted to form a larger terrestrial planet at Earth's location, or the debris may have been scattered by the gravitational perturbations of the neighboring worlds and simply added to the Solar System's store of asteroids and meteoroids.

On the other hand, had the trajectory been just a little shallower, the object would have missed altogether.

It is also important that the impacting object struck in such a way as to enhance the Earth's prograde direction of rotation i.e. rotation in the same direction as the planet's motion around the Sun. Planets are believed to have been built up from circumsolar material through the accumulation of smaller bodies or 'planetesimals' and their direction of rotation at the end of this accretion process is thought to be a legacy of the direction from whence the last major impacting body struck. Because these bodies are presumed to strike from random directions, the direction of a planet's rotation may be retrograde, as is, indeed, the case with Venus. However, it seems that the future development of a terrestrial planet will turn out very differently depending upon whether it rotates in a prograde or retrograde direction

Imagine a soft-boiled egg with a rigid shell, firm white and liquid yoke. If the egg is spun, the yoke will 'slosh' about. In a somewhat similar way, gravitational torques will move the solid portions of a rotating planet relative to its liquid core. The fluid motions of a planet's core can be greatly intensified when the motions of the liquid portion of the core resonate with one of the motions of the solid planet. This motion is converted, by friction, to heat at the core-mantel boundary, at the expense of the planet's energy of rotation. Simulations have shown that if the planet's direction of rotation is retrograde, more heat will be generated during a resonance passage and that this heat will tend to be released as volcanism, with the consequent release of greenhouse gases into the atmosphere and the resultant heating of the planet's surface. If tidal forces on the planet are relatively weak (as is the case for a planet without a large moon), its speed of rotation will decelerate only slowly, thereby increasing the length of time taken to pass through a resonance. The internal heating will be the more severe.

Tidal effects on planet Earth are much stronger than they would have been had the impact not occurred (or had occurred differently). The reason for this is another major effect of the collision, indeed, the one which caused astronomers to put forward the collision hypothesis in the first place. We refer, of course, to the Moon!

Earlier, we remarked how a mixture of terrestrial crust and material from the shattered impactor formed a ring around the early Earth. It is from this that the Moon is believed to have formed.

The Moon, as we have seen, plays a critical role in maintaining a relatively stable obliquity of Earth's axis. It is also largely responsible for the length of the terrestrial day. We already remarked that the giant impact which set in motion the processes leading to the Moon's formation would have increased the rotational velocity of Earth. Immediately following the collision, Earth was rotating significantly faster than it is today. Soon after the Moon accreted from the ring of debris, its distance from our planet would probably have been no greater than about 24,000 kilometers. Had there been oceans at that time, tides hundreds of meters high would have swept across the face of the planet, flooding all low lying land. At that remote epoch however, land tides—the flexing of the planet's surface under the powerful pull of a very nearby Moon—probably resulted in such heating of the Earth's surface as to melt the very rocks themselves.

Thanks to the prograde direction of rotation of the Moon as it orbited Earth, these tidal effects caused a slowing of Earth's rotation and pushed the Moon into an ever-larger orbit. This slowing of our rotation and recession of the Moon continues to this day. Currently, our day lengthens at a rate of two milliseconds per day per century, though this is not all due to the effect of the Moon. Solar tides also make their contribution to the gradual slowing of Earth's rotation and lengthening of the day. Nevertheless, the present speed of our planet's rotation and the length of its day is largely a balance between the increased rate of spin induced by the great impact and the subsequent breaking of this rate through the tidal effects of the Moon. Solar tides made only a small contribution to the length of our days.

It is a good thing that the Moon's orbit is prograde. Had it been retrograde, the tides that it raised on the early Earth would have caused a reduction, not an increase, in the Moon's orbital energy. In a relatively short time period, the Moon would have spiraled inward, crashing to Earth in a second catastrophic impact.

The possibility of a moon's orbit being retrograde is demonstrated by Neptune's giant satellite Triton. This object appears to be very similar to Pluto and is most probably a so-called Kuiper-Belt object captured by Neptune in the remote past. Triton orbits Neptune in a retrograde direction and is slowly spiraling toward it. Eventually, it will crash into the giant planet.

By now the perceptive reader will have noted that the Earth as we know it today was no foregone conclusion. There was nothing in the nature of the Solar System that predetermined the actual properties of the planet as it exists today. Indeed, the fact that Earth is as it is today, especially that it possesses the right conditions for the existence of complex forms of life, looks increasingly like the end result of a highly improbable chain of accidental events rather than the unfolding of a regular process of stellar and planetary formation. We read a great deal today in the popular scientific press about "habitable zones" and plans to search for terrestrial planets within the habitable zones of other stars. The inference (a reasonable one as far as it goes) is that if there is an Earth-like planet orbiting a Sun-like star within the habitable zone of that star; chances are good that it will be another home of life. Maybe even intelligent, technologically advanced life with which we could some day communicate.

However, from what we have been saying above, the habitability of our home world seems to depend more on the nature of a chance collision early in its life than with Earth's location within the Sun's habitable zone. True, the life-friendly results of the impact would have been, from the point of view of life, 'wasted' had the planet not been located within the habitable zone, but it could equally be said that they would have been 'wasted' had the planet been slightly larger or smaller or, for that matter, composed of slightly different combinations of elements.

The reader will also notice just how many 'chance' factors determined the exact nature—and outcome—of the collision. The mass of the impacting object, its trajectory angle, the stage in the history of Earth at the time of the event, even the initial velocity of Earth's rotation, apparently all played a role and probably needed to be within quite a small parameter range for the planet to develop as it did.

If we imagine that the process of planet formation is a regular one whose progress could in principle be predicted according to a relatively simple model, the Earth 'should have' turned out quite differently. Despite its position within the habitable zone, today it would probably have resembled Venus more closely than the "pale blue dot" that we know and love. Indeed, it is probably only an Earth-bound chauvinism that leads us to speak of "terrestrial planets" at all. Maybe a better name for these rocky worlds would be "Venusian planets", as it is quite likely that the majority of rocky worlds of similar size and gross composition to Earth and Venus experience conditions more reminiscent of those on the latter world. This is something to be remembered (but will most likely be forgotten!) during the burst of excitement and sensationalism that will surely erupt when the discovery of the first 'Earth-like world' orbiting within the habitable zone of another star is announced.

Putting aside our inevitable Earth chauvinism and life chauvinism, we could view the formation of the Earth as an orderly process leading toward the formation of another Venus that went wrong due to the impact of a stray planetary body. The Solar System's second Venus, as a result, turned out completely 'off-plan'!

Of course, the dichotomy of 'regular planetary development' vs. 'unpredictable accident' is an oversimplification. Planets accrete through the collision of smaller bodies, so being struck by these objects is actually a regular part of the process. Nevertheless, it seems that being hit by an extra large one is not a necessary part of the deal and it is the 'unfortunate' planets that are struck by the big ones that become the outliers of the population ...outliers in terms of properties, not necessarily in terms of position within the system.

The Solar System may have three such 'outliers' whose peculiar properties resulted from massive collisions early in the Solar System history.

Besides Earth, Mercury and Uranus have some anomalous features for which large impacts have been the suspected culprits.

The Uranian anomaly is its axial tilt. It is practically lying on its side as it orbits the Sun!

It is widely believed amongst astronomers that the most likely cause of this was a major collision with an object possibly as massive as Earth.

Mercury, the smallest of the true terrestrial planets, if we omit our own Moon, is anomalous in so far as it possesses an unusually large iron core. It is really a large ball of metal covered by a relatively thin coat of basaltic rock. Why should so small a planet possess such an abnormally massive core?

Some astronomers, for example Stuart Taylor, argue that the most reasonable explanation is for Mercury to have been initially a much larger planet that was smashed to pieces by a massive impact billions of years ago.[16] The dense core was not disrupted by the impact, but the outer mantel and crust were largely driven off into space, leaving behind an essentially bare core that subsequently became covered by a layer of rocky debris falling back from the collision. If this scenario is correct, the fact that Mercury has an oversized core and Earth an oversized satellite both tell of violent early impacts on these respective planets.

An early impact may even have left behind another Mercuric anomaly, the unusually eccentric orbit of this small world. Being the closest planet to the Sun, one would expect it to have the least eccentric orbit in the Solar System, but the truth is quite different. Mercury's orbit is even more elliptical than the relatively distant Mars. If it has suffered an early devastating impact, this might be another legacy of that event.

From this perspective then, the Earth's 'special' habitability can be thought of as analogous to the 'special' axial tilt of Uranus and maybe the 'special' oversized core and 'special' eccentric orbit of Mercury. They are all anomalies resulting from unusually large impacts early in the lives of these three planets.

Although more could be said along these lines, already a picture is emerging of a highly improbable series of 'co-incidences', some mutually related, some not, that has conspired to render this planet an unusually favorable place for advanced forms of life.

We can think of this in another way. Although we are far from knowing all the factors permitting Earth's habitability, and still further from ascribing numeric values to these factors, we will for the sake of argument pretend that we do possess this information and that we have prepared a graph in which each factor appears as a separate co-ordinate. Such a 'graph' cannot actually be drawn on graph paper as it will exist in a multitude of dimensions (each habitability factor being a separate co-ordinate and, therefore, a separate dimension). The multidimensional space that it delineates is simply a mathematical construction, not a real physical space. Assuming that we know each value for every habitability factor, we can conceptually draw lines in this hypothetical space from all of the co-ordinates. The location of Earth is where these many lines intersect. A change in the value of any of these parameters will result in a 'shift' within this 'space'. A change in the Earth's mass, for instance, would be marked as a shift in the planet's location on the graph.

We know that the point marked by the convergence of all these hypothetical lines is a habitable region of the 'space' delineated by the graph. We know this, simply because it is this point that locates our habitable Earth. What we would like to know, however, is the true extent of the habitable region of this 'space'.

At one extreme we could imagine a habitable region that encompassed the entire graph. Any combination of the graph's parameters would, in other words, provide an environment suitable for life. This would imply that life is essentially ubiquitous. Probably nobody has actually believed this, although William Herschel came close with his belief that life was so widespread in the universe that even the Moon and Sun (and therefore all the stars, one might suppose) harbored intelligent creatures. Today we might look back at the seemingly extreme views of this great astronomer and gently shake our heads, citing the eccentricity of genius together with the much poorer knowledge of the Sun and planets (and of living organisms themselves) in Herschel's day to excuse what would now be thought a thoroughly crackpot position.

What we are apt to miss however, is that Herschel was simply being a good Copernican! Aside from his belief in an inhabited Sun (a little extreme even for his day), most of his contemporaries would not have thought his opinions on the widespread cosmic presence of life eccentric. Most shared them, explicitly or implicitly as the logical conclusion of the Copernican position.

Indeed, if the Copernican position really was as fundamental as many wish us to believe, Herschel and his colleagues should have been correct. In other words, most of the graph's space should be habitable. We may actually see this as a test of the Copernican Principle; one that it clearly fails. The extent of that failure is acknowledged (even though we don't normally think of it in this way) by the fact that the opinions of Herschel and other early astronomers now appear eccentric.

At the other extreme, the habitable region of the graph might be restricted to a very tiny region effectively coextensive with the location of Earth itself. This would be tantamount to saying that if the values of any of the habitability factors differed by more than a miniscule amount from their actual ones, Earth would not be a habitable planet. In other words, if the position of Earth shifted ever so slightly on the graph, it would no longer be habitable. Similarly, if a twin of Earth was located in a slightly different position on the graph, it would not be capable of supporting life.

To some extent, it is empirically possible to judge whether the habitable region of the graph is closer to the first or second possibility. If it is closest to the first possibility, we should find that planet Earth has no special properties that are clearly seen as rendering it habitable. All (or most) planets should be inhabited and although we of necessity must be located on *some* particular planet, there is nothing other than pure chance to specify which planet that should be. According to this possibility, it is purely an accident of cosmic history that we are terrestrials living on Earth. We could just as easily have found ourselves on Mars. We could just as readily have been Jovians or even (had Herschel been correct) Solarians!

This would follow if Earth literally has no special properties rendering it habitable. It is the only possibility that is completely consistent with a thoroughgoing Copernican viewpoint. But it is utterly and conspicuously wrong!

By contrast, the other extreme understands the convergence of the actual values of habitability factors as being the only ones determining the habitable region. Any position only slightly displaced from this will lie outside of that region.

This is more than saying that the Earth lies at a unique point on the graph. Every point is unique, but if the habitable region is large, this makes no difference as to whether the Earth may or may not be deemed special with respect to life. What this second possibility is asserting is that it is precisely *this* location that delineates the extent of habitability. At this unique place, marked on our hypothetical multi-dimensional graph, and at no other, lies the zone of habitability.

This possibility is also open to empirical observation. It predicts that a planet will be habitable if and only if the values of all the habitability parameters exactly imitate those of Earth.

One way of testing this would be examining all the planets in the universe for the presence of advanced life. If any inhabited planets were found, the next step would involve determining whether these occupied the same region as Earth on the graph.

Another test would require changing the various parameters of Earth and seeing how far we could go before life became extinct.

Neither of these is technologically feasible, and there are some serious moral objections to the second as well!

Also, we are still largely ignorant as to all the habitability factors and to their actual values, so strict testing of the possibility is beyond our means.

Nevertheless, just as observational evidence has already ruled out the first possibility, and in so doing quite severely restricted the habitable region on our graph, so observational evidence already suggests that the habitable region is probably very small and may even be strictly constrained to the Earth's location on the graph.

The evidence to which we refer is precisely the many unusual factors that seem to make Earth a special planet. The Sun's unusual galactic orbit, the strange coincidences behind the remarkable matching of the apparent diameters of the Sun and Moon in our skies and the other odd coincidences that we have encountered all conspire to make Earth's place on the graph unique in an interesting way. As we earlier remarked, if all or most of the parameter range represented on graph was habitable, there is no reason to expect that we should find ourselves on Earth rather than on some other planet with widely different properties. But when we actually find ourselves on a planet that is marked out in some very peculiar ways, and when we have observational evidence that the habitable region of the graph is at least quite severely restricted, we must surely question whether this can be the result of pure chance. Chance seems too remote a possibility to be an adequate explanation and we must seriously wonder whether the very peculiarities that determine Earth's position on the graph space are also the ones that determine its habitability. If we picture, for a moment, the vast arena of this 'space' as an enormous wall on which the Earth's location is drawn as a tiny target, it is as we have scored an enormously improbable bull's-eye!

It is also interesting to note that the more we learn about habitability, the narrower the habitable region of the 'space' becomes. If this trend continues (and that is the way everything seems to be pointing at the moment) this alone provides a strong argument for a very restricted habitable region.

We might summarize this line of argument by saying that Earth's position on the graph is not only determined by the convergence of many factors, but that many of these factors themselves appear to be highly unusual and that this fact alone renders even their convergence highly improbable.

It is sometimes argued that this increasing restriction only applies to life forms that are either terrestrial or strict terrestrial analogues. This, in effect, sees our line of argument as being circular; terrestrial-type life can only exist in strictly terrestrial-like environments! Other forms of life, it is implied, may not have the same habitability requirements. Theirs might be equally narrow, but if there are many areas of potential habitability on the graph (even if each is itself very restricted) the sum total of the habitable regions may be quite large.

While this remains a possibility, there is no evidence whatsoever to support it. In fact, what evidence does relate to it is uniformly negative.

Life, it is argued, could break the terrestrial mould if it arose on a planet similar to the ancient Earth and subsequently evolved in a different direction as the planet itself evolved in a totally non-Earth-like way.

Both Mars and Venus provide good testing grounds for this idea. All three planets—Venus, Earth and Mars—are thought to have harbored quite similar environments in their youth, but have since progressed in three entirely different directions. If life appeared on each of them and if life is as adaptable as it appears to be on Earth, there is reason to think that well developed ecosystems should exist on these other two planets as well. In fact, even if life did not arise independently on Mars and Venus, material blown off the Earth by violent meteorite impacts in the stormy youth of the Solar System should have carried abundant biological material to our two neighbors. We could almost say that these neighboring planets *should* have thriving ecosystems if life inevitably adapts to its environment, even if it was not strictly indigenous to these other worlds.

All evidence suggests that neither planet possesses a thriving ecosystem; or any ecosystem at all for that matter. A microbial ecosystem in the upper atmosphere of Venus is a possibility that has not been sufficiently investigated to date (although evidence in its favour is underwhelming), but hopes for Martian life seem to be in constant retreat as our knowledge of that planet grows.

Another suggestion that is put forward from time to time involves the existence of life of an entirely non-terrestrial nature—silicon-based organisms living in lakes of molten sulfur for example. Once again, evidence that any such life may exist is totally lacking. Our radar images of the surface of Venus reveal no evidence that could be interpreted as forests of silicon trees and no silicon salamander has ever emerged from a hot spring here on Earth. More fundamentally, increasing knowledge of the chemistry of life has continually highlighted the unique nature of carbon as the molecule of life and water as the most suitable solvent. Silicon analogues of some organic (carbon chain) molecules do exist, but the similarity is confined to relatively simple molecular structures. Silicon rubber is one thing, but a silicon DNA analogue would be something of an altogether different order of magnitude!

It seems, therefore, that the habitable region of our graph is very restricted; that the value of the factors determining habitability fall within a very narrow set of limits and that a habitable environment will not occur unless there is a convergence within these narrow limits.

Thus far, we have not implied that the set of circumstances resulting in this anomalous set of habitability factors resulted from anything other than mere chance. The issue of a possible cosmic intelligence steering its course has not been raised. Nevertheless, the sheer remoteness of the probability that all of these factors could come together raises this issue in many philosophical minds.

To such minds, 'chance' has the appearance of an explanation based on ignorance. Are there, however, any persuasive reasons for believing that something other than chance is at work here? Is it more than a statistical fluke that we find ourselves on this cosmic freak of a planet? Is there, in short, evidence of what might be called a 'cosmic design' of which these strange coincidences rendering our planet habitable form a part?

To this fascinating question, we now turn.

Notes

1. Poul Anderson, *Is There Life on Other Worlds?* (London & New York: Collier-Macmillan & Crowell-Coillier, 1963), 87-90.
2. Ptolemy, *The Almagest* (R. Catesby Taliaferro, Trns) Great Books of the Western World (Robert Maynard Hutchns, ed. In Chief) 16 Encyclopaedia Britannia Inc. (Chicago, London, Toronto, Geneva, Sydney, Tokyo, Manila: William Benton, 1938), 10.
3. Galileo, "Sidereus Nuncius" quoted in Guillermo Gonzalez and Jay W. Richards *The Privileged Planet: How Our Place in the Cosmos is Designed for Discovery* (Washington DC: Regnery Publishing, 2004), 240.
4. Guillermo Gonzalez, "The Galactic Habitable Zone," Astrophysics of Life, M. Livio, I.N. Reid, W.B Sparks eds. (Cambridge: Cambridge University Press, 2005), 89-98.
5. Yu Mishurov and I. A. Zenina, "Yes, the Sun is Located Near the Corotation Circle," Astronomy & Astrophysics 341 (1999): 81-85.
6. Hernandez X Martos, M. Yanez, E. Moreno and B. Pichardo, "A Plausible Galactic Spiral Pattern and its Rotation Speed," Monthly Notices of the Royal Astronomical Society 350 (2004) L47-L51.
7. W.S. Dias and J.R.D Lepine, "Direct Determination of the Spiral Pattern Rotation Speed of the Galaxy," Astrophysics Journal 629 (2005) 825-831.
8. L.S Marochnik, "On the Position of the Sun in the Galaxy," Astrophysics 19 (1984): 278-283.
9. B.S. Balazs, "The Galactic Belt of Intelligent Life," *Bioastronomy—The Next Steps*, G. Max, ed. (Dordrecht: Kleuwer Academic Publishers) 61-66.
10. Dias and Lepine, "Direct Determination of the Spiral Pattern Rotation Speed of the Galaxy," 830.
11. Peter D. Ward and Donald Brownlee, *Rare Earth: Why Complex Life is Uncommon in the Universe* (New York: Copernicus, 2000), 208-212.
12. Gonzalez and Richards, *The Privileged Planet*, 8.
13. R. Kopp, Joseph L. Kirschvink, Isaac A. Hilburn and Cody . Nash, "The Paleoproterozoic Snowball Earth: A Climate Disaster Triggered by the Evolution of Oxygenic Photosynthesis," PNAS 102 (2005) 11131-11136.
14. Dave Waltham, "Anthropic Selection for the Moon's Mass," Astrobiology 4 (2004): 460-468.
15. J. Laskar, F.Joutel and P. Robutel, "Stabilization of the Earth's Obliquity by the Moon," Nature 361 (1993): 615-617.
16. Stuart Ross Taylor, *Destiny or Chance: Our Solar System and its Place in the Cosmos* (Cambridge: Cambridge University Press, 1998), 166-167.

Chapter 2
Signs of Design?

In the upper reaches of the Hunter River Valley in the Australian state of New South Wales, lies the tiny hamlet of "Wingen". Its name, apparently, means "burning" in the language of the original aboriginal inhabitants of the region.

This little village is notable for harboring two natural impostors!

Traveling up the Valley, away from the east coast, one may notice a road just outside Wingen leading to the "Burning Mountain", or Mount Wingen, from which the village derives its name. The 'mountain' is actually a hilly ridge from whose summit smoke, sulfurous fumes and (at times) flames belch from a number of fissures and small crater-like depressions. All around the 'craters' sulfur deposits coat the rocks and gained the reputation amongst early white settlers of the region for possessing medicinal properties. Enterprising locals even collected and bottled the sulfur for sale as a remedy for all types of ills in the manner of that other famed universal elixir—snake oil!

Not unsurprisingly, the pioneers who first settled the Wingen region looked upon Mount Wingen as an active volcano. This seemed a logical enough conclusion. After all, what else could it be? A hill topped by craters that continually spewed smoke and sulfurous fumes . . . ?

However, when geologists took a closer look at the mountain, a different picture began to emerge. To their surprise (and no doubt, bewilderment) the rocks near the craters and on the slopes were sedimentary. No igneous rocks could be found anywhere in the vicinity; a strange situation if the mountain had belched forth lava in the past.

Instead, what they found was clay that had been baked over many years into naturally occurring brick, and other evidence of a slow burning subterranean fire!

Eventually, the true nature of Mount Wingen became apparent. The region is rich in coal; coal which has high sulfur content. Thousands of years ago a surface outcrop of this coal was set alight, presumably by a forest fire or lightning strike. And the fire has been burning ever since!

During the passage of several millennia, the fire has slowly burnt its way through the coal seam, traveling underground along the ridge. As it burnt, clay soils were backed into brick and, in various places, surface soils collapsed into shallow 'craters' which allowed the smoke, fumes and (sometimes) even the fire itself to break through to the surface.

What appeared at first sight to be a volcano was actually something quite different. A naturally burning coal seam ... a hill literally on fire!

If a traveler's attention is directed opposite the burning mountain, he may notice a formation with a striking resemblance to a woman's face, poised on the rocky escarpment. This is the "Wingen Maid", dutifully marked on tourist maps of the region and well known to travelers.

Has someone carved a sculpture on the escarpment face?

No!

The Wingen Maid is no more a sculpture than Mount Wingen is a volcano. Both are, so to speak, impostors. They are not what they appear to be!

Despite her superficial appearance to a sculpture, the Wingen Maid is actually a natural rock formation, her features 'sculptured' over the centuries by the forces of wind and water. Although, from a distance, she may look as though someone has designed her appearance, this is nothing more than an illusion; a fortuitous combination of randomly formed markings etched by erosion into the rock.

Natural formations having the superficial appearance of design occur quite often and are not infrequently used to reinforce arguments purporting to prove that all appearances of design in nature are similarly explicable in terms of the interplay of blind natural forces. According to this line of reasoning, features such as these may mimic the products of designing intelligence, but this imitation is superficial only.

Actually, these 'designoids' (to borrow a term from zoologist Richard Dawkins[1]) are not totally divorced from intelligence; however the intelligence in question lies behind the eyes of the beholder rather than somewhere in the objective world. We speak of the pattern recognition inherent in the human brain. We all know how this can work overtime, reading apparent patterns into random noise as well as recognizing those that are objectively present. There is a potentially infinite collection of patterns which we can inadvertently project into white noise. As everybody who saw the film *A Beautiful Mind* will know, patterns can be seen in just about anything. The canals on Mars provide one good historical example of a design-like pattern read into random noise. Patterns in clouds provide a more homely one. If we were only capable of recognizing real patterns—there would be no Wingen Maid!

Yet, there are certainly instances of patterns—patterns indicative of intelligent design—inherent in external states of affairs which the human mind recognizes as intrinsic to those states of affairs themselves. However, it is not always easy to isolate the precise features that incline us to accept some states of affairs as products of design while continuing to reject others that appear superficially similar.

It is tempting to say that those states of affairs which show high levels of complexity are more likely to be recognized as design products.

However, this answer is flawed.

Some states of affairs display very high levels of complexity, yet would never be considered products of deliberate design.

A pile of leaves is a prime example of this. Whether deliberately raked together by a gardener or simply piled up against a wall over time by the force of the prevailing wind, a leaf pile is really a very complex state of affairs. If this is doubted, imagine a pile of hundreds of leaves being totally disrupted by a whirlwind and then try to picture the difficulty of reconstructing it such that each leaf is in exactly the same place and in the precise relationship with every other leaf as it had been before the whirlwind struck!

This level of complexity also implies that the probability of a leaf pile with these exact specifications having eventuated by chance is infinitesimal. However, it is infinitesimal in a way that raises no serious doubts that chance alone was operative. We are quite happy to accept that random forces alone were at work here. Any leaf pile must necessarily have *some* structure and the set of possible combinations of leaves is so vast that *whatever* structure eventuates will be highly improbable!

Conversely, consider an arrow painted on the concrete floor of a parking station. Compared with a leaf pile, this is a very simple state of affairs; at its most basic, it simply consists of an isosceles triangle joined to a rectangle, or even just a long strip of paint and two shorter ones angled to it. Unlike the leaf pile, if it was erased, one could replace it yin minutes. Moreover, the probability of such a relatively simple pattern emerging from chance is greater than the chance emergence of a specific pile of leaves. Yet, would anyone doubt that this arrow is a product of intelligent design?

Now, consider a watercourse. If this is simply gouged out of the ground (especially if it is winding rather than straight) it may be a natural creek bed. However, if it happens to be lined with concrete or wire-meshed pebbles, we would unhesitatingly conclude that somebody had designed it, at least in its present form. Maybe it was originally a natural creek bed, but we would certainly conclude that somebody had been involved in determining its present form.

Even if we found a winding watercourse—very similar in appearance to a natural creek—running through a public park or large private garden, we would still conclude that it had been artificially constructed (or at the very least, artificially altered) if we found it to be lined with wire-meshed pebbles.
Its meandering appearance would not fool us. On the contrary we would simply conclude that the landscape artist had designed it to look 'natural'. In other words, that it had been designed specifically to appear un-designed!

There are certain artifacts however, for which the presence of design can be very difficult to detect. I am thinking, in particular, of artificial rocks. If the garden landscaper is skilful, these may resemble natural rocks so closely that only a careful examination could detect the difference. Like the watercourse, they are designed to appear un-designed, but their designer may have performed his task so well that their true nature is not at all apparent.

But if it is not complexity per se that distinguishes a state of affairs as having been designed, what is it?

Mathematician and philosopher, William Dembski, argues that the twin aspects of complexity and suitable pattern provide the hallmark of design. A pattern is 'suitable' according to Dembski if it shows a requisite 'specificity'. If something displays both complexity and specificity—if it possesses (in Dembski's own words) "specified complexity" we can safely conclude that it is the product of design.[2]

The question is to isolate that which determines specification or specificity. Once again, the characteristic can be recognized more readily than it can be defined.

Mount Rushmore in the United States of America provides a good example of specificity. It is clear to anyone that the rock formations on this peak display patterns that no amount of erosion by wind and water could accomplish. Even if one did not know the likenesses of Presidents Washington, Jefferson, Theodore Roosevelt and Lincoln, one could still not escape the features of human faces displayed so accurately by the rock formations. Moreover, these patterns persist under changes of illumination and perspective, proving that they are objective and intrinsic to the rocks themselves and not something that is being projected by the human brain on a more or less random scatter of stimuli.

In this, Mount Rushmore differs critically from the Wingen Maid. Although the latter resembles a face under certain conditions, this appearance is lost upon greater scrutiny.

On several occasions the author has witnessed an interesting phenomenon of light from a small lookout on the Central Coast of New South Wales. Below the lookout, a rock shelf extending into the ocean is crossed by a number of small eroded channels and, typical of rock shelves within the inter-tidal zone of the ocean, has a very rough surface with many very small pools and ridges. About half an hour after sunset, and persisting until darkness prevents further observation, the appearance of a Mexican sombrero suddenly (literally *suddenly*) emerges from the surface of the rock. It looks exactly as if somebody had sculptured it into the shelf or, at the very least, that some natural pool had imitated art in a striking manner. Yet, at other lighting conditions, nothing remotely resembling a sombrero can be seen on the rocks. In fact, no single feature at all can be distinguished at the location of the phantom sombrero! It is purely an illusion of light and shadow caused by random formations of rock!

The sombrero, the Wingen Maid, the (in)famous Face on Mars and many other apparent examples of patterns may look convincing at first sight, but they do not stand up to closer scrutiny. They lack the specificity required by Dembski.

Secondly, if a pattern is to be accepted as indicative of design it must also be relatively independent of the state of affairs in question. It is possible, as we have said, to read just about any pattern into anything. This is a symptom of certain types of mental illness, but is also experienced by quite sane individuals who like to spot dog's heads in clouds or faces in flames. It not infrequently proves a trap for scientists who so desire observation to confirm their favorite theory that they 'cherry-pick' data points that appear to fit the pattern they expect (or hope) to find! Such patterns however, inevitably disappear as more data is amassed.

Dembski explains his notion of "relatively independent" by means of the following example.

He imagines that an archer draws a small target on a wall, stands back twenty meters or thereabouts, fires and hits the bull's-eye. From such a demonstration, we can correctly conclude that this is a person with considerable skills in archery. We could not conclude this if the target was large because, in that instance, anybody who could draw a bow would stand a good chance of hitting the bull's-eye. In other words, the small target (highly specified and tight) could be compared with Mount Rushmore while the large and easily-hit target would be analogous to the Wingen Maid.

Yet, suppose that the archer fired at a blank wall and, after the arrow had embedded itself, painted the small target with the bull's-eye centered on the arrow's position. This would give a match as tight as the first, but it would be pure fabrication and tell us nothing about the archer's skill; even though it might speak volumes about his honesty! The pattern would not, in that instance, be independent of the event.

Dembski's argument has much in its favour; however, we do not believe that it completely isolates the basic characteristic of design. In some respects it is too restrictive. For instance, by applying the criterion of specified complexity, it is doubtful if either the parking station arrow or the artificial watercourse in a landscaped garden would pass the test. Neither has a pattern as specified as, say, Mount Rushmore. The painted arrow would still be recognized as having been designed even if it was very rough and ready and, as we have already said, the level of complexity in both arrow and watercourse is quite low.

Is there some other property or set of properties by which designed states of affairs can be distinguished from those which lack design?

We will argue for a different approach to the issue shortly, but first let us consider a fallacious argument that has been spawned by the assumption that design essentially equals complexity.

The argument to which we refer is one used by Dawkins and others in their effort to demonstrate that random processes, if continued for a long enough time, will eventually produce something that appears indistinguishable from design. In particular, they employ this argument to try to prove that the genetic code could have arisen by natural selection without any need for the influence of a designing cosmic intelligence.

The specific issue of a cosmic intelligence will be taken up later. For now we are only concerned with characterizing design itself, without raising questions as to who or what might be the designer in any particular situation.

The argument to which we refer is usually presented in some variation of the following form.

Suppose we had a very large number of monkeys randomly playing with the keys of an equally large number of computer keyboards. Given sufficient time, so the argument runs, they should produce a copy of the *Encyclopedia Britannica*.

The basic assumptions of this argument are;

i. The appearance of design is a matter of complexity, and
ii. large numbers and long periods of time will eventually give rise to the required level of complexity.

Our version of the argument will be more modest. We suppose (for the sake of argument) that the monkeys playing with their keyboards produce, nothing quite so ambitious as an entire encyclopedia, but simply a single article giving instructions on how to build a toy electric motor.

Now, suppose that you found such an article (maybe within the encyclopedia that the monkeys were supposed to have written!) and you followed its instructions to the letter ... and the little motor ran perfectly!

What would you then conclude about the author of the article?
Logically, whatever else you may conclude about him, you would be forced to the conclusion that he knew what he was talking about ... that he was (relative at least to yourself before you read the article) an expert in the science of electric motors and their construction. And this would further imply a sufficient knowledge of the history of the subject, a good acquaintance with the technical terms used ("armature" and so forth) and at the very least, a working knowledge of electronic circuitry. Needless to say, all of this requires an intelligence of the same order as the article's reader.

This is, as philosopher Richard Taylor argued, a logical inference.[3] The article is clearly something that appears to have been written by an intelligent person, providing instructions for the construction of a device requiring a certain level of knowledge and skill. But it does more than *appear* to fulfill these criteria. It actually *does* fulfill them. The article actually accomplishes the task for which it appears to have been designed. To accept this (which we must do if we built the motor and it actually worked!) and yet to deny that the article was intelligently designed would be, as Taylor argues, irrational.

In short, if we are told that doing X, Y and Z will result in A happening and if we do X, Y and Z and A does happen, we normally conclude that whoever provided the instructions knew his subject. This is common sense for most people.

It may—at a stretch—be possible to argue for the simian authorship of an article that apparently gave instructions for the manufacture of something that was either impossible to construct or that simply did not make sense. This could logically be dismissed as simply 'monkey business' (though, quite frankly, only a very desperate person would try to argue this way in practice) and its appearance to an intelligently designed article nothing more than a designoid fluke. But this avenue of argument closes—even granted that it was ever really open—once the article is found to carry information that proves to be valid. In other words, once the article is found *to point to something beyond itself*. This last phrase is emphasized as its importance will be apparent in a little while.

Before we leave our monkeys, let us suppose that, instead of having been given keyboards to play with, they were simply given building blocks. Now, suppose that from these blocks, they constructed a flight of simple stairs that enabled them to climb out of the observation area and flee back to the forest. Would we conclude that this staircase was the result of random arrangement of the blocks? Or would we rather conclude that the monkeys were sufficiently intelligent to see the possibility of using the blocks in a simple construction capable of facilitating their escape? If we could see a purpose in the monkey's actions, would we not conclude that they had actually *designed* the simple staircase for the very purpose for which they used it?

Once again, the hallmark of design is demonstrated by whether the suspected design points to a larger state of affairs beyond itself, i.e. whether it serves some purpose or fulfils a function for which it appears to have been constructed.

Transitive Complexity

The propensity for a designed state of affairs to point beyond itself is, we argue, the major defining characteristic of such states.

In the study of grammar, one meets a vague analogue of this property, and a quick look at this may help to clarify the point we are making. In studying verbs, the grammarian distinguishes between those verbs which are known as 'transitive' and those which are not. Transitive verbs are defined as those which "take a direct object, either expressed or implied". For example the verb "saw" cannot be used in a sentence unless it has an object. We cannot simply say "I saw" and expect to convey sufficient information. The question remains "What did we see?"

"I saw the man", "I saw that my attempt at humor had fallen flat" "I saw that he was not interested in my proposal" and so forth. Even stating something like "I looked and I saw" has an implicit reference which (presumably) will be understood by the hearer in that specific context.

On the other hand, "I live" or "I think" require no further reference. When the French philosopher Rene Descartes set forth his famous theorem "I think, therefore I am" he did not have to explain what he was thinking about. "I think", meaning that he had the capacity of thought, was sufficient. Unlike "saw", these latter verbs do not require an object; they are not transitive.

We argue that just as transitive verbs point to something beyond themselves and cannot be understood unless this object is specified (either implicitly or explicitly), so those states of affairs which most clearly manifest design point beyond themselves to a broader picture in which their existence is explained. Like transitive verbs, they are directed toward an object. With deference to the grammarians, we suggest that the name "Transitive Complexity" (TC) be given to these states of affairs and we propose that it is in the *transitivity* of a state of affairs that design is most readily recognized.

Let us review our earlier examples of designed states of affairs in the light of the criterion of TC.

Consider first the parking station arrow. The main reason why this is assumed to be a product of design is its obvious role in directing traffic in a certain direction; towards the next deck of the parking station, or toward the exit or the lower deck, which ever the case may be. It is not because of any high level of complexity, or even because it displays evidence of artistic or design skill on the part of the person who painted it. In fact, it could be very poorly painted and very simple. Even a single ribbon of paint, broader at one end and narrowing down to a point, would probably suffice for the intended purpose. All that is needed is for information regarding the destination of the particular traffic lane in question (for instance, whether it leads to the upper storey or to the exit) to be conveyed accurately to the motorist for the arrow to be recognized as having been painted at that position for the fulfillment of its designated purpose. And if that perceived purpose is indeed fulfilled, it would be irrational for the motorist to conclude that the arrow had not been deliberately placed there for that very reason.

We suggest, therefore, that the main reason for concluding the arrow to have been intelligently designed is its transitive nature, not its complexity per se. The simplest of painted arrows are just as clearly the products of intelligent design as are marvels of architecture or computer programs! We will return to this point shortly.

It is clearly evident that in this example, the 'pointing beyond' involves the provision of information. The provision of information is also of paramount importance in Dembski's examples of specified complexity. Indeed the information criterion is often seen as being essential for determining whether something has or has not been designed by an intelligent being. It is undeniable that information frequently is the factor determining the presence of absence of intelligent design, however there are instances where the transfer of information is not involved and yet design is clearly present. Our earlier example of an artificial watercourse is one such instance. Let us look a little more closely at this.

We assume that the watercourse has been designed in a landscaped garden specifically to imitate the circuitous rout of a natural creek bed, but we have also assumed that a stone and wire mesh bed and sides have been substituted for natural rock and that it is in their presence that its artificial nature is most clearly revealed. This too is transitive, though not for the same reason as the painted arrow. We cannot say, as we did with the arrow, that the watercourse exists for the purpose of conveying information to the observer. It is clear, nevertheless, that it has been constructed for a purpose and a little thought shows that it is actually serving two quite separate functions, namely, carrying away excess water and (probably of greater importance in many landscaped gardens) providing an aesthetically pleasing setting.

A critic may pounce upon the first of these purposes as being quite adequately fulfilled apart from the necessity of intelligent design. After all, there are natural watercourses that fulfill this role with complete adequacy!

The critic could quite correctly point out that a natural watercourse also points beyond its own existence—in effect, that it has a purpose, and that this purpose is the same as the first one given for the artificial watercourse. They both serve to carry away excess water.

However, in the case of the natural watercourse, this function has been caused directly by natural processes ... by the water itself initially spilling down a line of least resistance and eventually eroding a channel in the soil. The process could be explained completely in terms of physics; gravity, erosion and the like. With Dawkins in mind, we could term this 'designoid' rather than 'design'.

A natural watercourse might also be located within a garden or park as to induce a very aesthetically pleasing effect. However in that instance, it is more likely that the park or garden was landscaped so that this natural feature was included within the overall design, rather like Dembski's example of the archer who first fired his arrow into a blank wall and then drew a target around it.

In the case of the artificial watercourse however, these natural processes have not been at work, as is evidenced by the foreign material with which the watercourse is lined. Such material does not occur naturally in these places and its presence cannot be explained by the same processes that we used to account for the existence of the watercourse's natural counterpart. Moreover, the artificial watercourse—by its very artificial nature—is not in a place that a natural one would be.

We have no trouble explaining the existence of the natural watercourse, and its features, in terms of physical cause and effect; of water running downhill, erosion and so forth. On the other hand, neither the existence nor the features of the artificial watercourse can be explained as easily. Some other factor is clearly implied; and this 'other factor' involves the whole situation in which this watercourse occurs. It involves, that is to say, an explanation as to why the garden exists and why it has been constructed in the manner in which we find it.

This other factor is not difficult to find. It is the intelligent planning of the garden landscape in which the artificial watercourse has been given a specific place. It is, in a word, *design*. Design is not the cause of the artificial watercourse, in the way that water erosion is the cause of the natural one, but it could be called the *reason* for it. Without this design, neither the artificial watercourse nor the landscaped garden of which it forms a part would exist.

Consider again the example of the article supposedly written by monkeys. We are now in a better position to see the absurdity of this. An article is a clear case of TC. It exists solely for the preservation and transmission of information about some state of affairs existing beyond it. Of course, for this to be possible, the author of the article must have knowledge of that state of affairs—the 'subject' of the article. He/she must also possess the requisite knowledge of grammar and language in general to enable this information to be adequately expressed. An article is not simply a jumble of words that could be strung together by random processes such as monkeys playing with keyboards. The letters and words themselves are almost incidental to the meaning which they are intended to convey. That meaning remains whether the words themselves are written in English or Arabic. The letters and words are, in reality, a code. The very existence of the code—any code—is determined by the information it carries. Its existence is intrinsically purposeful and goal-directed. It exists solely for the purpose of encoding the requisite information. What the hypothetical example of the article supposedly written by monkeys attempts to do is accept the existence of the code and affirm its success in having correctly encoded the information, while denying its purposeful nature. It is in the recognition of this contradiction that gives the example its sense of the absurd.

Although we have been using the term "Transitive Complexity", thus far we have been speaking about transitivity rather than complexity per se. "Complexity" is a relative term. Any state of affairs is, by its very nature, complex to some degree. It is in this broad sense that we are using the word here. As we have already stated, some of these transitively complex states of affairs are in reality quite simple. The degree of complexity is low in the case of the painted arrow, somewhat higher in the artificial watercourse and higher again in a written article. It is much higher in, say, an advanced computer program, but that does not necessarily mean that the computer program will be more readily recognized as a product of design than an article in a book or, for that matter, the painted arrow on the parking station floor. Each of these states of affairs has transitivity and (a degree of) complexity and it is in the recognition of this combination, not in the degree of complexity per se, that design is identified.

Something having a very high degree of complexity will *ipso facto* have only a small probability of being put together by random processes. Yet, design is not validly inferred from a high level of complexity alone. We remarked earlier that the degree of complexity exhibited by a pile of leaves is such as to render the precise combination of leaves in any particular pile a very improbable occurrence. Yet we do not on this account assume that the leaf pile has been designed. The fact is that *any specific* leaf pile will be a low-probability occurrence, but given the right conditions of wind currents etc., a leaf pile of some kind is virtually assured. The complexity of a leaf pile is not indicative of transitivity. It seems to be, as we might express it, without purpose. Moreover, any pile is as good or bad as any other; they are all equally without *specification*, to use Dembski's terminology

On the other hand, the degree of complexity cannot be overlooked entirely.

We might recall that in our example of the natural and artificial watercourses, we remarked that the natural watercourse may have the superficial appearance of purposeful design. This raises the question as to whether we can be in error about transitivity; whether a state of affairs can mistakenly be judged transitively complex or a genuine instance of TC erroneously dismissed.

The possibility of error must, to a certain extent, be admitted. We humans can be as fallible about this as anything else!

Not long ago, the author noticed a rather unusual cloud formation. It was at a time when the concept of TC and the paradigm case of the painted arrow was uppermost in his mind, which was probably why his attention was drawn to the formation in the first place. A small group of clouds came together to form an almost perfect arrow shape, but what was even more unusual was a tiny cloudlet just off the end of the 'arrow' (though clearly disconnected from it) and, as near as could be discerned from the quite considerable distance of the formation, in direct line with it. In short, the cloud arrow 'pointed' directly at this tiny dot of a cloudlet. Could this be classified as an instance of TC?

Some cloud formations do display TC and are deliberately designed. They are advertising products written in the sky by pilots trained in the art of skywriting. It is not uncommon to see, just prior to polling day, "Vote for Joe Smith" or whomever, written across the sky. Clearly, this displays TC if there is an election in the offing and if somebody named "Joe Smith" is a candidate. We would even assume that it was an act of skywriting if there was no election or nobody by that name in the political scene. We might then be puzzled as to the motive of the skywriter, but a cloud formation bearing so many striking similarities to real political advertising of the vaporous kind, would not be doubted as the work of such a person.

Nobody, however, could have mistaken the cloud arrow and its apparent target for skywriting. The formation persisted for only a very brief while and, more importantly, comprised just one tiny part of a much larger mass of broken clouds that revealed no overall pattern or apparent purpose. There was really no temptation to think of this 'cloud arrow' as having been an exercise in skywriting. It was only something that, for a brief moment, bore some superficial resemblance to skywriting. There may have been a certain resemblance to transitivity in the fact that the 'arrow' appeared to point (how ever briefly) to an object—a cloudlet not visibly connected to the 'arrow'—but, besides being only a fleeting appearance, this 'pointing' lacked any purpose.

Why should this tiny cloudlet have attention drawn to it in this way?

No reason at all!

Moreover, the cloudlet was not really something 'beyond' the 'arrow' except in a very superficial sense. They were both parts of the same general cloud formation. It would have been more impressive if the 'arrow' had pointed to some unusual feature of the landscape (the highest hill within the field of view, for example), although even this would not be sufficient to prove genuine transitivity. After all, a cloud shaped like an arrow much of necessity 'point' to something. Chances are high that another cloud will be in line with it if we look far enough and, if not a cloud, some feature on the land's surface will convincingly line up. No doubt, if we tried sufficiently hard, we could find something interesting about what ever feature to which the 'arrow' pointed!

If, on the other hand, we saw a clearly defined arrow of cloud pointing downward toward a mountain that we knew to be Mount Townsend and if, above the arrow, we saw written in the clouds "This is Mount Townsend", we would clearly have an instance of transitivity. In that case there would be no doubt. A skywriter with knowledge of local geography would surely be at work!

Following the first global images of Mars from a Mars-orbiting spacecraft, there was a flurry of excitement in certain quarters when the top of one of the mesas was found to bear a striking similarity to a face. The 'Face on Mars' was popularized by a small minority as providing proof that Mars had once been inhabited, or at least visited, by intelligent alien beings. Clearer images of the mesa from a later generation of Mars-orbiters, however, revealed the markings to bear little resemblance to a human face. The pattern of erosion scars revealed in these later images bore no resemblance to the products of intelligent design. Nevertheless, although no serious scientist ever believed the 'Face' to be a genuine artifact, it is interesting to note that some of the arguments put forward by its supporters actually involved what we have termed TC. 'Face' supporters were quick to point out that a group of hills in the same general region bore some resemblance to pyramids and that another region looked somewhat like the ruins of a great city. Of course, there are many pyramid shaped hills on Earth that owe nothing to ancient Egyptians or Mexicans and how many natural products of erosion are known as "The Lost City"? Yet, the 'Face' supporters claimed more than the mere existence of these features. They attempted to demonstrate certain alignments between the 'streets' of the 'city' and the 'Face', arguing that these were so arranged as to point to the feature (so that the Martians could constantly see the 'Face' from the streets of their 'city'?).

In other words, the 'Face' supporters tried to prove their point by looking for TC in some way associated with it. This is a subtle admission that the apparent design-like appearance of the 'Face' was not of itself sufficient proof of artificiality. If it could be associated with something that not only looked as though it had been designed ('streets' of the 'city') but actually fulfilled a purpose which pointed beyond itself (somehow became associated with the 'Face') design, and therefore alien intelligence, would become the only rational conclusion.

Their logic was impeccable. What was at fault was their data, and that is why they failed to convince anyone who was not already a believer in the 'Face'. What they really needed to prove their case was an example of TC as tight as the above hypothetical example of a skywriter drawing an arrow in the sky pointing toward, and naming, a specific geographical feature. Yet, all they really found was an example analogous to the cloud arrow that, briefly and from a certain perspective, seemed to point to an isolated and very transitory cloudlet. What they found may have superficially appeared to exhibit transitivity but only if viewed with the eye of faith. Moreover, any semblance of transitivity which may have been imagined vanished, together with the 'Face' itself, as more accurate imagery of that region of Mars became available.

We conclude, therefore, that states of affairs clearly exhibiting TC logically must have been designed by an intelligent agent.

The converse, however, is not necessarily correct. Intelligent design does *not* necessarily involve transitivity. It is possible to have a product of genuine design that is not transitively complex. For instance, an artist doodling on a paper napkin may draw a human face that bears no intended likeness to anyone known to him. It is not a portrait, it does not represent any specific person—nor did the artist have any conscious purpose in drawing it. It was simply a doodle. But it was obviously the product of intelligent design and would immediately be recognized as such. In Dembski's words, it possesses specified complexity.

We suggest that this specified complexity is, however, recognized as indicative of design because it has previously been observed as characteristic of situations that *have* been transitive. *This* particular drawing may not have any purpose and may not represent any particular person. But we *have* seen similar drawings that have been designed for the specific purpose of representing particular people. *These* revealed TC, and we argue that it is in the recognition of comparable features in the 'mere doodle' that causes us to conclude that it is also the product of intelligent design. Had the person drawing it not been an artist, the result may have possessed such scant resemblance to a human face as to cause this conclusion to be doubted. In that instance, we may have decided that any resemblance to a face was no more compelling than the Wingen Maid.

We suggest that, although instances of design not involving TC are certainly found, the design inference in these is not as logically compelling as in situations where TC is apparent. Moreover, we suggest that such inference as does exist in the former is dependent upon comparison of relevant properties of the design suspect with similar features of other situations where TC *was* evident. Therefore, although nobody would in point of fact deny that the artist's doodle was the product of intelligent design, this conclusion lacks strong logical implication. A badly drawn doodle could be rejected, unlike a badly drawn directional arrow, for which design is strictly implied while ever transitivity is fulfilled.

In concentrating on TC, therefore, we admit that genuine instances of design will probably be missed, but we believe that this is an acceptable price for maintaining this logically stricter criterion.

TC and information transfer in codes
Although it is too restrictive to equate transitivity with the transfer of information, as the artificial watercourse example demonstrates, the most obvious and striking instances of TC are surely those that do involve such a process. We argued earlier that an informative article is a clear instance of intelligent design and that any explanation which fails to do justice to the purposeful nature of the article is both irrational and illogical. This conclusion follows, of course, irrespective of the language employed by the writer. Moreover it continues to apply even where the 'language' being used is another type of code; for example, a computer code.

Indeed, a code need not be as specific as an article in an encyclopedia to demonstrate clear transitivity and, therefore, intelligent design. The SETI program is essentially a search for the existence of intelligent design amongst a great deal of random noise. Yet, most SETI enthusiasts do not necessarily expect to receive an alien transmission yielding great quantities of information; though they would surely be delighted if that is what they found! Their quest would be considered successful if they discovered a signal, obviously originating well beyond the bounds of our own Solar System, containing within itself a clear indication of having been put together by a thinking being.

But how could they determine this?

We may recall the burst of excitement in 1967 when Cambridge University graduate student Jocelyn Bell detected a regularly pulsed signal in radio telescope data. So regular did the pattern appear that Bell actually dismissed it as 'scruff' or manmade artificial pollution from a satellite or other distant transmitter. It seems to have been her supervisor, Anthony Hewish, who first recognized the signal as genuinely astronomical (which probably explains why Hewish subsequently received more credit than Bell for the discovery) and that some new type of object had been located. The question was however, *what* kind of object?

So rhythmical, so precise, did the signals appear that the new radio source was unofficially and only half-facetiously dubbed 'LGM-1'; 'LGM' standing for 'Little Green Men'!

One scientist at the time jocularly remarked that the radio astronomers may have listened in to the heartbeat of a cosmic man.

Two early hypotheses were put forward in all seriousness. The first suggested that the pulses might somehow be generated by an ultra-dense object known as a neutron star. Such bodies had been hypothesized as the remnants of certain types of supernova or exploding stars. Briefly stated, these stars collapse inward until the material at their core becomes as dense as an atomic nucleus. The rest of the star is blown to pieces by the shockwave of the core collapse, leaving behind an object as massive as the Sun but small enough to fit within the CBD of a moderate sized city. Theoretically, these objects should be rapidly rotating and may have extremely strong magnetic fields associated with them. It was hypothesized that some mechanism involving these magnetic fields may generate a beam of powerful radio waves radiating from the neutron star. As the latter spins on its axis, the narrow 'pencil' of radio waves sweeps through space similar to a lighthouse beam. According to this scenario, the pulses detected by Bell and Hewish marked the passage of this beam across the dish of their radio telescope. Until that time, no neutron star had been discovered and prior to the Bell/Hewish announcement, even those who believed that such things existed were not optimistic with respect to their discovery in the foreseeable future. Others doubted that such objects existed at all.

The second suggestion was that the Cambridge team had found an interstellar beacon placed at some location within the Galaxy by a highly advanced space faring civilization. It was thought to be a sort of interstellar lighthouse or navigation beacon for the benefit of interstellar spaceships.

As it turned out, subsequent discoveries of similar objects—some of them clearly associated with supernovae remnants—clearly supported the first alternative. We now know that these spinning neutron stars—called pulsars—are not at all rare within the Galaxy; and all are entirely natural!

Now, suppose that you are a radio astronomer and that, like Bell and Hewish, you discover a pulsed radio source that is obviously at stellar distances. But in your case, the pulses are not at all regular. On the contrary, they come in groups of varying length with short but clearly determined pauses in between. You note that each successive group is longer (contains more pulses) than the preceding one until the sequence ends in a longer pause, only to begin again with the shortest group. You then realize that the pulses are giving the sequence of the first five prime numbers, repeated over and over again with relatively long pauses in between.

You would undoubtedly conclude that this was no pulsar; but genuine ETI! Why?

Not because you had deciphered some alien code yielding information too advanced for our generation of scientists to know. Not because you had been given information about the history of an alien race. The information given to you *in the signal itself*—the first five prime numbers—was nothing you did not know already. What *was* significant was that you deduced, from the nature of the signal, that the *cause of the signal also* knew this information. From this fact you correctly concluded that the signal had to be the product of an intelligent mind. Only intelligent minds can know about prime numbers and design a signal which announces this fact to anyone capable of receiving it.

Such a signal does not *primarily* reveal TC through its information content. Rather, it demonstrates it by evidencing a purpose for which that information had been transmitted. That purpose is not to teach about prime numbers, but to effectively broadcast the message "We are here—we exist!" This is accomplished by pointing to some regular feature of nature (prime numbers in this hypothetical example) which could be discovered by any intelligent life form, anywhere in the physical universe, whose mind functioned in an approximately similar manner to the sender's. The design of the signal points beyond itself to a being of similar mentality to the one who deciphered the message.

Sir Fred Hoyle, as well as being one of the most brilliant and controversial cosmologists of last century, was also a skilled writer of science fiction and one of his stories *A for Andromeda* became a television series in the early 1960s. In this story, a new radio telescope with state of the art sensitivity picked up a signal from the Great Galaxy in the constellation Andromeda which, from its structure, was quickly recognized as being artificial. This one, however, carried more information than a simple series of prime numbers. It encoded instructions which, when deciphered, enabled scientists to construct a super computer, having a capacity far in excess of anything that humanity alone was capable of constructing at that time.

Suppose that something akin to this were actually to happen. Suppose that a radio astronomer really found a cosmic radio signal that, when deciphered, contained a code for the construction of something that had previously been beyond the capabilities—and the knowledge—of humanity. Because such a signal obviously possesses a high level of both transitivity and complexity, no reasonable person would doubt its intelligent origin. Indeed, doubting it would, as already argued, violate the very process of reason itself.

Now suppose that the coded information for the construction of this fantastic device was found, not in a radio signal from outer space, but on information recorded on a piece of tape found by the roadside. One may quite reasonably doubt that this had come from another planet, but there would be no doubt whatsoever that it was the product of an intelligent mind; probably not alien, but maybe (depending on the exact nature of the information) a foreign government think tank or some secret research program carried out in our own country.

Further suppose that this information was found, not on a macro-sized tape, but recorded on a nano-device; encoded on a single very complex molecule. The logic of the situation has not altered with the decrease in size. The coded instructions remain coded instructions and continue to demand an intelligent mind as the only logical explanation for their existence. The only major difference is the new requirement that this intelligent mind must have a mastery of nanotechnology far beyond the capabilities of contemporary humanity!

This latter example is the one which actually places the most stringent demands on the intelligent mind involved. The hypothetical aliens in the first example need not be very far advanced of humanity, unless they really were located in another galaxy like Fred Hoyle's Andromedids. Humans have already beamed a message to the stars in the remote chance that somebody or something is out there listening (a very remote chance actually, as the message was beamed toward a globular star cluster where habitable conditions are extremely unlikely!)

The second example does not require any advanced technology, only clandestine research by someone secretly producing a device unknown to the general scientific population.

However, the third example requires the ability to manipulate matter at a molecular, even atomic, level. Because the few faltering steps taken by humanity in this direction have yet to carry us very far, a discovery such as that envisioned here would necessarily involve intelligence beyond the human.

Surprisingly, although the first two examples were purely hypothetical, the third is not. Scientists really have found nano-coded molecules of extreme complexity. Moreover, the messages they carry yield both the blueprints and the means of construction for the most complex entities in the known universe; something far more complex than the fictional supercomputer of *A for Andromeda*!

We refer to the living cell and to the DNA molecules which carry the code for its construction.

DNA and the code of life
How can a molecule, how ever complex, carry the code of life?

Before attempting to answer this, let us look more closely at the DNA molecule itself.

DNA is a long threadlike molecule of enormous complexity; a chain of atoms of indefinite length. It is composed of units—like 'links' in the chain—each consisting of sugar, deoxyribose phosphate and a 'side group'. The latter is always one of the four bases namely, adenine (symbolized as 'A'), thymine ('T'), guanine ('G') and cytosine ('C'). A complete unit consisting of base, sugar and phosphate is called a nucleotide. Therefore, a molecule of DNA is really a chain of nucleotides.

Now, it has long been known that any given protein has a fixed sequence of amino acids, and that these DNA sequences can, as it were, spell out 'words' consisting of similar sequences of nucleotides in an alphabet of four letters, A, T, G and C.

The mystery of how DNA replicated was not cracked until 1953 when Cambridge scientists James D. Watson and Francis H. C. Crick discovered the now-famous double-helix structure of the molecule; a structure which has been picturesquely likened to that of a double spiral staircase with two rails. The 'rails' are each composed of alternating units of sugar and phosphate whereas the 'steps' are built from the four nucleotide bases themselves.

These bases happen to be very particular about their associates. They will only pair off in a very narrow range of combinations. Thus, an A is always found with a T and a G with a C. It is this restriction (which seems only a curiosity at first glance) that holds the key to determining the manner in which the DNA double-helix copies itself and, therefore, to one of the basic features of life itself.

The replication of the DNA molecule is one of the most wonderful phenomena in the universe, yet the mechanism behind it is, in principle, marvelously simple. Essentially, the double-helix 'unzips', freeing each half of the helix to combine with any available free units and become a template for a new chain. This, at least, is what happens in broad terms. We now know that the double helix does not simply 'unzip' of its own accord. There is a tiny molecular 'cutting machine' which runs along the molecule and facilitates the unzipping; a piece of naturally occurring nano-technology that displays a high level of TC.

However, because of the abovementioned restriction governing the pairing of bases, the only free units with which the unzipped DNA molecule can become attached will be those matching its earlier partners. That is to say, in the original (unzipped) molecule, we have the combinations A-T, T-A, G-C and C-G as the only possible combinations. Upon unzipping, A parts from T, T from A, G from C and C from G in the above sequence, and are thereby freed to pick up other units that were not parts of the original molecule. But, because their choice of possible partner is severely restricted, the new sequence can only be A- (new)T, T-(new)A, G-(new)C and C-(new)G. In other words, the new sequence will be a copy of the original. Both strands of the unzipped molecule will, therefore, end up as halves of a new double-helix exactly copying the original. The DNA molecule has replicated itself.

Thanks to this phenomenon, the genetic code for each species is passed on down through the generations as each organism replicates after its own kind.

The four-letter alphabet of DNA is not, however, the only code vital for life. There is also the protein code consisting of 20 amino acids which the DNA alphabet must produce.

The mystery of how the DNA code accomplishes this feat was solved by M. Nirenberg and colleagues, who found that three bases code for one amino acid. Thus, the four-letter DNA alphabet yields a possible 64 three-letter words, 61 of which code for the 20 amino acids while the remaining three act as 'full stops' signifying the end of a protein chain.

The manner in which DNA is actually translated into protein is, however, somewhat involved. The DNA, with its four-letter code is translated into another form of nucleic acid known as ribonucleic acid or RNA. The A, G and C remain unchanged during this process, but the T is replaced by uracil ('U'). In a process known as transcription, the nucleotide sequence of the DNA is first of all copied into the nucleotide sequence of a particular type of RNA known, not surprisingly, as 'messenger RNA' or mRNA. Strands of mRNA consist of fairly short chains (about one thousand nucleotides in length—'short' in the present context) which code for single proteins. At transcription, one of the strands of the DNA double helix is copied into RNA. The helix is first of all unwound (which, as we have already mentioned, involves the action of a molecular machine specially fitted to unzip the molecule) and one of the strands directs the synthesis of an RNA polymer having a complementary nucleotide sequence. The transcription of mRNA is carried out by a complex of proteins known as RNA polymerase.

This, at least, is a brief account of basic mRNA synthesis as it occurs in its simplest form; namely, in bacterial cells. In more complex organisms, the situation is complicated by the occurrence of intervening sequences or introns, which separate the coding sequences. In these higher organisms, the initial RNA transcript is subjected to a process during which the introns are removed and the coding sequences spliced together into a molecule of mRNA.

Following its transcription, the mRNA moves from the nucleus of the cell, into the cytoplasm, to the site where decoding of the message takes place. The translation of the mRNA is carried out by a complex set of molecules, including complex globular organelles known as ribosomes. These are aggregates of around 50 proteins together with three chains of RNA. A ribosome attaches itself to the strand of mRNA at a spot on the molecule known as the ribosome binding site. This location, usually close to one end of the mRNA chain, contains a 'start' triplet of AUG or GUG.

During the process of translation, the mRNA passes through the ribosome, in a manner that has been likened to a length of magnetic tape passing through the recording head of a tape recorder. It is at this point that another type of RNA needs to be introduced; interesting molecules that act as a set of transducing elements relating each triplet in the RNA (that is to say, each unit of the code) to the particular amino acid being coded for. The molecule responsible for this is known as transfer RNA or tRNA, and consists of about one hundred nucleotides folded into a looped structure. Its shape is not unlike that of a hairpin.

As the length of mRNA passes through the ribosome each triplet section, in its turn, associates with its appropriate tRNA, which also carries the appropriate amino acid. This amino acid molecule is removed from the tRNA strand by special proteins within the ribosome and added to the growing amino acid chain. In this way, the amino acid chain is built up one acid at a time as successive tRNA strands carry their attached amino acids to the ribosome. When the amino acid chain—the protein molecule—is completed, it is detached from the tRNA and folded by other molecular devices into the three dimensional shape appropriate for its specific function.

The amount of information capable of being stored and carried in and by these molecular codes, and in particular by the DNA code, is staggering to contemplate. Using the convenient information unit of the binary digit or 'bit', we are able to gain some idea as to just how stupendous the capacity of the genetic code really is. The 'bit' is a single piece of information which is given as either a 'yes' or a 'no' and is normally written, for the sake of convenience, as 1 for 'yes' and 0 for 'no'.

Now, it so happens that those two possible 'bits' can code alternatives supplied by the nucleotide bases. These may now be written as; adenine = 11, thymine = 10, guanine = 01 and cytosine = 00.

Consider, now, the DNA of a bacterium. This is the shortest of the strands and as such carries the least amount of information of any DNA. But just how much information *can* it carry?

One could answer this by pointing out that a strand of bacterial DNA is composed of some ten *million* nucleotides or twenty million bits. If we printed this out in full, using the letters A, T, G and C, it would fill several thick books!

But that does not really answer the question. We would still like to know how many different coded genetic messages could be written by utilizing all possible combinations of the letters printed in these hypothetical books.

Merely giving a number would, however, do little to help us appreciate just how vast the possibilities really are. The number would simply be too large to comprehend.

As an exercise, consider all the atoms comprising all the stars, planets and whatever else may exist, in the visible universe. Think about this for a moment. Try to imagine how many atoms there are in the book you are holding. Then picture the volume of the Earth in comparison with this book and once again try to form some impression of how many atoms there might be in that.

Then recall that the Sun is about a million times more massive than the Earth. How many atoms are there in the Sun?

But the Sun is only one of around three or four *billion* stars in our galaxy. And our galaxy is but one of a *billion* galaxies in the observable universe. How many atoms in *all* of this?

Remarkably, the answer has been calculated, at least in order-of-magnitude terms. You can write it down if you wish. Take a large sheet of paper, write down the number *one* close to the left-hand side and then follow it with 78 zeroes.

This is a large number by any standard. But compared with the number of possible coded messages available to the DNA strand of a bacterium, it is quite literally next to nothing.

To write down that number, the 'one' would need to be followed, not by a 'mere' 78 zeroes, but by *six million* zeroes!

If we were to write out this number longhand, at the rate of one zero each second, it would require ten weeks to complete the task! Yet, this fantastic number of possible coded messages refers to the *shortest* of the DNA strands. It is the *least* number of possible coded messages carried by a DNA molecule!

In higher forms of life, a single DNA molecule may be comprised of as many as 300 million individual atoms and, if fully extended, would measure several centimeters in length.

Such is the amazing complexity of life!

Yet, it is not just a question of complexity per se, but of the form that this complexity takes. It is not simply that the nucleic acid bases can form such an enormous number of combinations, but that these combinations really act as codes through which information is carried. It is not simply that we have found molecular books containing so many letters as to potentially write vastly more words than there are atoms in the observable universe, but that these 'words' really do say something of significance and the 'books' in which they are written contain instructions from which living organisms are made. What we encounter is TC of a profound order.

Moreover, it goes without saying that the very great range of potential combinations made possible by this immense complexity renders the chance occurrence of something functional highly improbable to say the least. Sir Fred Hoyle and Professor Chandra Wickramasinghe estimated that the probability of producing just one gene by chance alone is as small as 10^{-100}; a probability so small as to be "entirely ruled out" as the product of randomness.[4] These authors predated the growing Intelligent Design Movement of recent years, yet the issues they raised were very similar to those of concern to these later writers. Their conclusion, namely, that some sort of intelligence is at work in nature, was also similar. However it is noteworthy that they did not draw theological conclusions from this. In this way they also agreed with some (though certainly not all) of the Design Movement proponents. This fact exposes the claim which is not infrequently voiced by orthodox Darwinists (namely, that anyone proposing design is a fundamentalist Creationist in disguise) as simply ludicrous!

Certain structures associated with life display other remarkable properties at the molecular level. We refer specifically to the amazing 'biochemical machines' which biochemist Michael Behe highlighted in his controversial book *Darwin's Black Box*. Possibly the best known of these is the bacterial flagellum—in effect, a nanoscale outboard motor which propels the organism through liquid. But the occurrence of biochemical machines is actually widespread and essential to life at its most minuscule dimensions. We have already mentioned in passing that the unzipping of DNA strands themselves is accomplished by a tiny 'motor' running along the double helix. Molecular biologists now know of systems of pistons, cogs, pulleys, rotating shafts—just about every mechanism that we may imagine—existing at the molecular level!

Yet, it was not the complexity of these systems per se that impressed Behe. What excited his interest most was the fact that systems such as this, if they are to operate at all, must have each of their constituent parts functioning and in its correct place. Take the common mouse trap for example. This is far simpler than most of these biological molecular motors in so far as it possesses fewer working parts. Nevertheless, if one of these parts is missing or damaged, the mouse trap will not work. Similarly the flagellum, will fail to function if one of its components is missing. Such systems as these possess what Behe terms "irreducible complexity". In short, they had to be 'all or nothing'; either complete or completely non-functional.

Behe argued that this raised difficulties for the theory that such structures evolved through the process of natural selection. He correctly pointed out that natural selection can only occur between systems that are more or less efficient at fulfilling a certain task. The 'best' is selected for as against the 'merely good'. But even the 'merely good' must have previously been selected in favour of a less efficient (though still essentially functional) system. It is not a case of a working system being selected in favour of one that cannot perform the task at all.

Yet, for an irreducibly complex system, this choice of selection does not exist. As already noted if a system of this nature lacks only one component part, it is not merely rendered less efficient; it becomes absolutely useless. And useless systems do not evolve through natural selection!

Behe concluded that these irreducibly complex systems must have come into being in their entirety, as quantum leaps so to speak. They could not have arisen by evolving from simpler systems through the step-by-step process of natural selection, as the intermediate steps would have been non-functional and as such, selected against. Moreover, as these systems appeared specifically fitted to perform the function that they did in fact perform, he concluded that they must be the products of intelligent design. In this he implicitly recognized the existence of TC. Indeed, each example of irreducible complexity is also an example of TC. It would not be an exaggeration to say that Behe's irreducible complexity represents a special—and very interesting—subset of TC!

We may add that a further level of transitivity is present here as well, namely, the fact that the blueprint for these molecular machines is written into the code of the DNA molecule. If we could believe that monkeys playing with keyboards could by accident hit upon a computer code for the construction of a new type of nano-scale electric motor plus the nano-scale set of devices enabling its construction, we might find it slightly more credible that natural selection was the only mechanism at work here, but that surely involves too great a leap of irrational faith!

Evidence of Design?

The complexity of life's chemistry (upon which we have only touched) is one of the factors causing some scientists and philosophers to rethink their naturalistic assumptions. A primary example of this change of mind is the philosopher Anthony Flew. Flew, whose 1950s work *God and Philosophy* had become almost a 'scripture' of atheism, had long opposed belief in any kind of cosmic intelligence. Yet, in the early 2000s, he came to embrace a position not unlike that held by the Design theorists. The evidence for design in biochemical systems played a major role in his change of view.

Evidence of intelligent design in terrestrial life does not automatically imply the working of intelligent design in the universe as a whole however. It is just possible (though, we must admit, highly unlikely and completely unsupported by evidence) that a naturalistic intelligent design may be responsible for terrestrial life. The most plausible possibility would be intervention by intelligent aliens. Could the Earth be someone's nursery?

Let us say immediately that there is no empirical support for this notion, although it is a theoretical possibility. The strongest objection, apart from lack of evidence, is the way that this hypothesis leads naturally into an infinite regress. Thus, if life—biological organic life or, maybe, artificial life originally constructed by biological organisms—is required to explain terrestrial life, then how did *this* life arise? And if this earlier generation of life requires an even earlier one, then how did *that* generation arise?

If the regress is stopped at any point, we must be prepared to answer the objection as to why it could not have been stopped at first base; before it got started, i.e. with terrestrial life itself.

We may be reminded of the rhyme

Little fleas have lesser fleas
Upon their backs to bite 'em
And lesser fleas still lesser fleas
And so ad infinitum.

There is, however, one important difference. The actual existence of "little fleas" is not dependent upon the logically prior existence of "still lesser fleas". If fleas really did have fleas and so on, that would be interesting, but it would not alter the fact of the existence of fleas. Neither does the non-existence of "lesser fleas" mean that "little fleas" do not exist. But in the above regress, each level depends for its very existence upon there being a next-order level. The regress is not merely infinite (which would be bad enough as it raises the sticky issue of numerical infinity) but is also, as philosophers say, "vicious".

Another discovery of modern science that opens the possibility of intelligent design on a cosmic scale has raised an even more direct challenge to straight naturalism, and has caused a number of scientists to rethink their commitment to the metaphysical assumptions of naturalism and materialism. We refer to the fine tuning of the environment of Earth and indeed of the universe itself. Evidence from a number of sources increasingly reveals a world so fine-tuned that only a small change in the basic properties of the universe, or a minor alteration in the laws of physics, would render life as we know it impossible on Earth and, very likely, throughout the cosmos. We have already noted in the previous chapter many of the exquisitely delicate balances that must be maintained for Earth to be the friendly place that we inhabit.

Nevertheless, this latter argument is not sufficiently tight to provide a secure foundation for so radical a thesis as cosmic intelligent design. Without further evidence, one may argue that the fine tuning apparent in both terrestrial and cosmic environments reveals nothing more than the *appearance* of transitivity; a closer analogy of the arrow-shaped cloud than of true skywriting. It may seem, from our unavoidably biocentric perspective, that all of these apparently fine-tuned features of Earth and the wider universe have been put in place for the purpose of life, and especially of intelligent life. But skeptics argue that this is looking at the issue from the wrong end. It may be argued that it is only because the universe, or the Earth within this universe, possesses such fine-tuned characteristics that we are here at all to observe it. This, we remember, is the Anthropic Principle which we met in the previous chapter. To be more specific, it is the form of the AP known as the Simple Anthropic Principle (SAP). This does not assert that our presence somehow caused the universe to be the way it is (although some more complex versions of the Anthropic Principle have ventured into this swampy metaphysical territory). It merely asserts that if the universe did not possess certain properties—i.e. those that render it habitable by intelligent life—we would not be here to observe it. Since life is extremely complex, any environment permitting its existence will necessarily involve a complex interplay of factors that will give it the appearance of fine tuning. This, the skeptics argue, is just another instance of patterns being read into random data. Moreover, the appearance of pattern is made even more likely in this instance because the random data is itself very complex and the number of possible patterns already severely constrained by the requirements of habitability. If the SAP is given as the last word on the subject, the universe is not obviously transitive. Certainly, it appears as though it exists (or at least, has the features which it possesses) in order that intelligent life may flourish, but this is just the appearance of transitivity, not the reality. It is simply a more complex example of the cloud arrow apparently pointing to an isolated cloudlet.

Nevertheless, not everyone agrees that the SAP should be given the last word on the subject. The fine tuning evidenced by the SAP continues to cry out for explanation. Many scientists worry that supporters of the SAP are effectively endowing it with causal efficacy and they see this as preventing any further search for real explanations of fine tuning. They are not saying that the SAP is wrong; only that some of its supporters are loading it with a burden that it was never intended to carry. It should be remembered that the SAP at its most basic level is essentially a restatement of common sense. It simply states that, for us to exist at all, the universe must possess properties making it habitable, or, in its more specific applications, the Galaxy or our region within it, the Solar System or Earth must have habitable properties. Our existence *requires* this, but does not *determine* it in any causal sense. The SAP does not attempt any causative account as to why these habitability factors exist. It cannot perform the task the skeptic asks of it. It simply states that our existence necessitates a certain convergence of factors having taken place, but it leaves this convergence itself unexplained. As it stands, it neither supports nor denies the existence of design.

One could, therefore, answer the skeptic by arguing that the SAP depends on the universe having been the product of design; that the apparent transitivity is real after all and that a universe designed for the purpose of bringing forth intelligent life is precisely one in which the SAP *should* be valid. And of course, anyone arguing this may very well be correct, but that conclusion is no more self-evident than the skeptic's assertion.

If design is to be placed on a more secure footing, the apparent transitivity must be shown to be *real* transitivity and alternative explanations of fine tuning invalidated.

Life in a 'megaverse'?
The chief alternative explanation argues that the realm we experience as 'the' universe is actually just a tiny part of the whole. The universe in its entirety, according to this model (of which there are several varieties) is really an ensemble of 'universes'. Ours is merely one of a possibly infinite number. It is further supposed that each of these will differ to a greater or lesser degree from each other, even to the extent of having different laws of physics. According to this thesis, the SAP is valid, not because the universe has been specially designed but because ours is a member of a small subset of universes in which conditions are suitable for life's existence. In effect, the argument states that if one progresses through all possible values of all the parameters that determine the nature of a universe, eventually one will hit upon a set that is suitable for life.

According to this hypothesis, universes may exist where the force of gravity is thousands of times stronger than in our own or where the velocity of light is different. But we know that altering the value of basic parameters in this way has ramifications for the whole of physics. Altering the value of the force of gravity seriously affects stellar evolution, to name just one example. If the requirements for life are as tight as they appear to be, a universe with parameters only a little different from those of our own would be rendered uninhabitable. Therefore, if life is to exist at all within the megaverse, it must of necessity inhabit a universe where the parameters are fine tuned for its existence. However, this fine tuning will merely be a selection effect, not the product of deliberate design.

Although this argument is a popular one, it encounters a number of serious difficulties.

Firstly, we have no real reason for thinking that our universe is indeed part of a 'megaverse' of alternative universes. Even if this is true however, it need not automatically follow that each universe is fundamentally different from any other. Therefore, it need not follow that all possible *types* of universes (i.e. universes with different physical laws or different values of basic parameters) exist in the megaverse. Even if a megaverse does exist, its component universes might all be similar to our own, with respect to general properties if not specific features.

Secondly, explaining a phenomenon by appealing to a hypothetical megaverse does not obviate an explanation in causal terms. In this respect, the megaverse model has no more explanatory value than the bare SAP.

In fact, it faces a philosophical problem similar to that of using ultimate causes to explain specific events. For example, if asked in a chemistry examination why hydrogen and oxygen combine to form water, the answer "Because God wants it to happen" would not be sufficient. A theist would undoubtedly agree and the answer might indeed be relevant in a theological discussion, but the chemistry teacher wants an explanation in terms of something a little more immediate!

Likewise, our hypothetical chemistry teacher would not find the answer "Because we live in one of the universes within the megaverse where this happens", any more satisfactory.

Consider the following example.

Suppose a wing falls off an airplane as it climbs toward maximum altitude. This is (fortunately!) a rare event, but one that certainly has a finite probability of occurring. A committed megaverse believer could point out that because of this finite probability, even though the event may have a very low chance of occurring in this universe, the probability of its happening an infinite number of times in an infinite ensemble of universes is unity. We experience it because ours just happens to be one of the universes in which it occurs.

But would this 'explanation' satisfy the flight inspectors?

We think not!

The cause of the accident must be found within this universe, and the question as to whether this situation, or infinite variants thereof, occurs in an infinite ensemble of other universes is hardly relevant.

Many presentations of the megaverse model fall foul of the so-called 'gambler's fallacy'. A tossed coin has a 50% chance of coming up 'heads', *each time it is tossed*. The gambler's fallacy is the assumption that if the coin is tossed a sufficient number of times, the probability of its coming up heads somehow increases. But this is simply not true. The probability of the coin coming up heads is exactly the same for the one thousandth toss as it is for the first—50%. Moreover, if a thousand gamblers are each tossing a coin, the probability that the toss of any one specific individual will come up heads is not affected. It remains 50%, irrespective of whether only one person is tossing the coin, or whether there is a casino crowded with gamblers. Similarly, if something has an essentially zero chance of occurring in our universe, it continues to have an essentially zero chance of occurring irrespective of whether ours is the only universe or just one of a megaverse. What we need to know is the nature of the causal chain that brought the phenomenon in question about and the wider set of conditions under which that causal chain occurred. In the present example, the flight inspectors will want to have an explanation in terms of metal fatigue and the like, or even whether there were any signs of intentional tampering with the wing of the aircraft.

Once the possibility of intentional tampering is raised, the issue is taken to a new level. If, for instance, it was discovered that several small explosive devices, designed to detonate with falling atmospheric pressure, had been attached to the wing (how the pre-flight inspection missed these is left to the reader's imagination!) intentional interference would immediately be concluded.

The alternative 'multiple universe' explanation would run something like this: Because there is a remote but finite probability that bombs designed to detonate upon reduced air pressure can self assemble by chance, in an infinite ensemble of universes this process must occur an infinite number of times. Therefore, although the probability of it happening in any particular universe is extremely small, the fact that it *did* happen in ours proves that we inhabit one of the very rare universes in which conditions are suitable for this highly improbable process to occur. There is therefore no need to suspect terrorist activity. The appearance of intelligent interference is purely an illusion!

I cannot begin to imagine the reaction of the crash investigation committee if presented with this as a serious report! That many scientists unquestioningly accept a parallel account of the even more complex phenomenon of life is a matter of concern.

The reader will undoubtedly note the close parallel between the above and the monkeys-with-keyboards example discussed earlier. Both examples begin with a phenomenon that displays a high degree of organization. Similarly, this organization is of a kind which appears to be directed toward some goal or objective; an article yielding information in the one instance and the destruction of an airplane in the other. Moreover, each has been so organized that the respective goal is achieved. In each instance, it is the *anticipation* of the goal that determines the nature of organization of the state of affairs intended to reach it. The author of an article determines what information he wishes to convey in the article and chooses the words best suited to that end. The saboteur determines how he can most efficiently destroy the aircraft, and plans his strategy accordingly. There is in each instance a sort of 'feedback' from the desired goal. However, at the time this feedback plays its crucial role; the goal itself does not exist. The feedback is therefore not from the goal itself, but from the *anticipation* of the goal; the plan conceived in an intelligent mind.

It is the recognition of this last fact that exposes the absurdity of explaining away either example in terms of random events.

Similarly, the quest for an adequate explanation as to why our world is so remarkably suitable for the existence of complex life will need to include as many details as possible about the way in which it came into existence and about the forces that fashioned it. If an account in purely physical terms appears inadequate or contrived—in the manner of the hypothetical aircraft crash investigation—the quest must also take seriously the possibility of 'intentional tampering'. Intelligent design does at least offer a causal explanation in a way that the megaverse model does not. For that reason alone, it must be considered more scientific. If this statement is doubted, let the reader imagine that he is a member of the committee investigating the air crash. Imagine that two reports were tabled giving alternative explanations as to why the tragedy occurred. One report concludes that the presence of pressure-sensitive bombs proved the crash to have been an act of deliberate sabotage. The other presents the megaverse explanation summarized earlier. Let the reader himself consider which he would favour as the most reasonable and 'scientific' explanation!

We might also remark that the megaverse model ultimately fails to explain the high level of cosmic fine tuning. If there really is an infinity of universes, each one differing slightly from the next, there should be universes (indeed, an infinity of universes!) that are just sufficiently fine tuned for life, but lack the exquisite uniformity of law that our universe demonstrates. We may extend this even further and recognize that there should be universes fine tuned for life, but not for discoverability. Although the full force of this will become more apparent later, we may also add that there should be other universes which are both habitable *and* fine tuned for discovery, yet totally lacking the beauty of the basic physical laws demonstrated by our universe. In short, even if the megaverse model did have some validity, at best it could only present arguments as to why we live in a habitable universe, not why we live in one where (as we shall see in Chapters Three and Four) habitability, intelligibility and beauty, so remarkably harmonize at basic levels of physical reality.

According to the most megaverse models, the individual universes within the megaverse are assumed to be autonomous. The laws of physics operating within them are such as to prevent one universe impinging upon another. However, if the megaverse literally includes universes of every possibility, there is no *a priori* reason for believing that this restriction should apply. Indeed, there should be infinitely many universes in which the laws of physics are such that they do not remain autonomous. But if this is true, what prohibits these 'invasive universes' from swallowing up the entire megaverse in some sort of multidimensional chaos?

There is no logical impossibility involved here. Postulating invasive universes is not like postulating universes in which there exist square circles or formless bodies—logically impossible non-things which 'exist' only as meaningless juxtapositions of words. But if logical impossibility alone prevents the existence of a universe in the megaverse, the existence of invasive universes should logically be implied by a thoroughgoing megaverse cosmology. If this reasoning is sound, the existence of an infinite ensemble of universes in which all possibilities are fulfilled, is therefore found to strongly conflict with observation. Clearly, we do not inhabit (nor *could* we inhabit) a multidimensional cosmic chaos!

If we are correct in our assessment, the megaverse model fails to provide an adequate explanation of fine tuning. We argue that the alternative hypothesis of intelligent design is a more reasonable and more scientific one that better explains the data. This conclusion would, however, be strengthened by the discovery of further evidence of TC in nature. If nature is the product of intelligent design, TC should be widely evident, though not necessarily obvious to a culture trained to seek explanations only in terms of mechanical processes.

We suggest that such indications of TC would be evident if the fine tuning that permits the existence of living organisms also produces an environment in which one class of those organisms is enabled to fulfill certain basic desires; desires which in themselves do not seem to have been determined by the biological struggle for survival

Stated thus, we admit that this sounds obscure. Nevertheless, the thought is really quite straightforward, even though few people (even amongst scientists and philosophers) seem to have entertained it, let alone seriously contemplated its scientific and philosophical ramifications.

Yet, the more we seriously think about them, questions such as the following are revealed as increasingly profound;

Why is nature intelligible to the human mind?

Why can we have knowledge at all?

Why are we located in a part of the universe that enables observation out to cosmic distances?

Why is an atmosphere suitable for life also one that allows observation of the distant universe?

Why is the human brain of sufficient complexity to enable the performance of mathematical calculations sufficient to describe (at least approximately) physical reality?

Why does the human race possess a desire for knowledge and understanding that goes far beyond the requirements for biological survival? (And)

Why is Nature so accommodating that this desire can be sated?

Why do we possess a sense of beauty and a capacity for experiencing awe?

Why do we desire the contemplation of beauty? (And)

Why is Nature so benevolent as to provide the means of satisfying this desire?

At first sight, these types of question may seem void, but behind them lie deep issues which are so habitually ignored that even the bare recognition of their existence requires a radical shift of thought.

Many of these issues, especially those concerning the intelligibility of the world, were masterfully tackled by Guillermo Gonzalez and Jay Richards in their book *The Privileged Planet*. This appears to have been the first work specifically dealing with the subject in depth. An occasional mention had been made previously by the odd scientist or philosopher, but mostly by way of aside during discussion of another topic.

By following s similar line of argument to that of the previous chapter, Gonzalez and Richards conclude that life at the human level can exists on this planet only because Earth is anomalous. These anomalies reveal themselves in the form of certain phenomena that are unique within our own solar system and which are probably extremely rare or even non-existent within the wider universe.

The authors then show that many of these anomalies do more than simply enable Earth to be inhabited by intelligent creatures. They also provide the means by which these same creatures can discover fundamental facts about the universe. These anomalies therefore, not only permit the existence of intelligent life, but also render nature intelligible to that life!

There is no *a priori* reason why this should be so. There is no *logical* reason why the only places suitable for intelligent life were such as to absolutely preclude all knowledge of a wider universe. How wide would our knowledge of the world be if we were troglodytes confined to deep underground caverns? But if the nature of the universe was such that intelligent life could only exist underground, that is exactly what we would be!

We will look at the Gonzalez/Richards argument; however we will also go beyond their position to another equally telling phenomenon. We shall argue that the anomalies allowing this planet to be inhabited by intelligent beings and which (*a la* Gonzalez and Richards) render the universe intelligible to these creatures, also provide these same creatures with means to satisfy their thirst for beauty and, ultimately, to be inspired by a sense of the awe-full. Gonzalez and appreciation, both of which appear to be, to borrow a Richards argue that the anomalies of our planet provide us with both a home and a platform of observation from which the universe is rendered intelligible. We argue that they also provide us with a gallery of the beautiful and ultimately what we may call a temple of the Awe-full.

It will also be argued that neither a platform of discovery nor a gallery of the beautiful would be of any use to a race which did not possess the twin passions of curiosity and aesthetic phrase coined by Aldous Huxley, "biological luxuries"[5] i.e. features that are not essential for the survival of the species, but which nevertheless add a deeper—in a sense, more 'spiritual'—dimension to life. Huxley originally used this term to describe humanity's advanced sense of color, which appears to be developed beyond anything required for pure biological survival, but the term is equally applicable to a wide range of human abilities. Yet, while these may be luxuries from a purely biological or, if we may so express it, 'animal' point of view, they are necessary aspects of the truly human character; they are part of what makes us human.

We shall endeavor to show that many of the anomalies that ensure our safe home in the cosmos are also responsible for phenomena of a beautiful nature, ultimately transcending beauty and touching upon the deeper sense of fear and awe. We see it as no coincidence that it is the experience of awe that arouses (but ultimately leaves unsatisfied) our deepest passion; the sense of the Transcendent.

It will be further argued that, because there is no *a priori* connection between the provision of a home for intelligent life and a set of conditions where these 'biological luxurious' desires can be fulfilled, a transitive complexity within our environment is implied. We further note that there is no reason to think that nature should be constrained to provide fulfillment of these desires, unless that constraint is placed upon it by an intelligence that transcends nature and fashioned it according to this very purpose. We suggest that the existence of features in nature that arouse a sense of awe, yet which leave this sense unsatisfied, also provides evidence suggesting a Transcendent designer who has so arranged both the world and human psychology to lead us ultimately to find satisfaction for our very deepest aspirations beyond nature; in the Transcendent himself.

Notes

1. Richard Dawkins, *Climbing Mount Improbable* (New York: W. W. Norton, 1996), 6.

2. William Dembski, *Intelligent Design: The Bridge Between Science and Theology* (Downer's Grove, Ill: InterVarsity Press, 1999), 127-139.
3   .Richard Taylor, *Metaphysics* 2nd. edition (Edgewood Cliffs, NJ:Prentice-Hall, 1974), 117-118.
4. Fred Hoyle and Chandra Wickramasinghe, *Living Comets* (Cardiff University College: Cardiff Press, 1985), 109.
5. Aldous Huxley, *The Doors of Perception & Heaven and Hell* (Harmondsworth: Penguin Books, 1959), 24.

Chapter 3
Our Privileged Planet

Following the publication of Ward and Brownlee's *Rare Earth* in the year 2000, a new phrase has entered the lexicon of scientific speculation. The "Rare Earth Hypothesis" is more than simply an idea postulated by a pair of scientists. The fact that it continues to be so widely discussed, rather than dismissed out of hand as it surely would have been just a few decades ago, signifies a revolutionary shift of intellectual attitude. This is more than an agnosticism concerning intelligent life on other planets. It is a shift from a position that assumes Earth to be typical to a more realistic one recognizing the great diversity of planets, and the very real possibility that Earth, and therefore complex life itself, represents the anomalous rather than the typical.

The Privileged Planet Hypothesis

In a sense, Ward and Brownlee prepared the way for the even more radical ideas of Gonzalez and Richards; or what might be termed the "Privileged Planet Hypothesis" (PPH).

The authors of the PPH sum up their position as follows;

> The myriad conditions that make a region [of the universe] habitable are also the ones that make the best overall places for discovering the universe in its smallest and largest expression.[1]

To do full justice to the arguments by which they arrive at this conclusion would require the reproduction of their book; something which is hardly appropriate here! We hope, nevertheless, to present a clear outline of their position without becoming lost in the finer details. The PPH is nevertheless foundational to the line of argument presented here as well as being of great significance in its own right. It is strongly recommend that the reader acquaints himself/herself with this very important work.

'Perfect' solar eclipses

We have already remarked upon the remarkable 'coincidence' of the apparent size of the Sun and Moon as seen from the surface of the Earth. That two astronomical objects of such diverse size, nature and distance should match so perfectly in their angular (or apparent) diameter is a truly remarkable fact frequently noted in elementary books on astronomy.

However, as already remarked, this correspondence is mostly dismissed as simple coincidence; an 'explanation' which we argued is too simplistic and ignores the stringent anthropic considerations that place these severe restraints upon the apparent diameters of both bodies.

Our present interest — and one to which Gonzalez and Richards called attention — concerns just one of the consequences of this correspondence of apparent diameter, namely, solar eclipses.

There are three types of solar eclipse.

First, partial eclipses, as their title implies, occur when only a portion of the solar disc is obscured by the Moon. Unless a partial eclipse is very deep (that is to say, unless the Moon actually covers most of the solar disc) or the event has been widely publicized in advance, solar eclipses of this type tend to pass unnoticed by the general population.

Annular eclipses are also, in a sense, partial in so far as the entire disk of the Sun is not obscured. They differ, however, from the type mentioned above by being *central*, i.e. by having the Moon pass directly across the solar disc. In this respect they more closely resemble total eclipses, but differ in that the Moon fails to cover the entire solar disc. In annular eclipses, the Moon appears as a solid black circle surrounded by the brilliantly glowing ring of solar disc; hence the term "annular" . . . from "annulus" or "ring".

Annular eclipses occur because the apparent diameters of the Sun and Moon each varies slightly. Thanks to the slightly elliptical orbits of the Moon around the Earth and of the Earth around the Sun, the distances of these objects vary slightly and this in turn causes slight variations in their apparent diameters.

This third type of solar eclipse is by far the most dramatic.

As we mentioned, both total and annular eclipses are central, so called because the Moon passes across the centre of the solar disc. By contrast, partial eclipses are not central; at least not from any locality on the surface of the Earth. An observer outside the path of a central eclipse will likewise see the Sun only partially obscured. Of course, the path of visibility of the central phase is much narrower than the track of the partial phase of the same eclipse.

What we do *not* observe on Earth are super eclipses in which the Sun and most of the solar corona vanish behind the disc of a huge eclipsing body. Eclipses like this occur on the moons of Jupiter, where the distant Sun vanishes completely behind the giant planet. For such eclipses to be observable on the Earth however, either the Sun would need to be dramatically smaller or more distant, *or* the Moon to be much larger and/or orbit our planet a lot closer than it does. As we saw earlier, any of these alternatives would be bad news for complex terrestrial life.

Nevertheless, these anthropic considerations do not completely eliminate the element of coincidence in the remarkable similarity of the apparent sizes of Sun and Moon. One may argue that even if it be granted that there are very good anthropic reasons why the Sun must appear essentially the size that it does *and* even if it be further granted that there are equally sound anthropic reasons why the apparent diameter of the Moon is likewise strongly constrained, there remains the coincidence that these two sets of anthropic constraints should conspire to produce such a striking correspondence in apparent size. Why, in other words, should the physics of the universe not be such that anthropic considerations dictate a Moon one degree in diameter and a Sun only one quarter this size?

For that to be true however, many basic physical parameters would need to be altered.

For instance, if the Moon's apparent diameter was conspicuously larger, gravity would need to be weaker for Earth not to be subjected to tremendous tides. However, a weaker gravity would in turn require a larger Sun, if it was to maintain a level of nuclear burning sufficient to maintain habitable temperatures on Earth. The Earth also would need to be larger to hold a sufficient atmosphere for life to flourish. In the wider universe, weaker gravity would result in profound changes in the evolution of stars and even in the expansion rate of the universe itself.

In short, a weaker gravity universe would almost certainly be one without life. But the point being raised here is that there appears to be no *a priori* reason why this should be so—why life *should* require the physical conditions that it does; conditions that tightly constrain the apparent diameters of Sun and Moon.

This is the remaining 'coincidence' which, as we can see, strikes at the fundamental properties of the universe itself.

According to the PPH, the fact that we, at the Earth's surface, can observe total solar eclipses in which the solar disc is barely (though nevertheless, completely) covered by the Moon—that is to say, what Gonzalez calls "perfect eclipses"—not only exemplifies this strange anthropic coincidence, but also opens an important window of discovery to intelligent life on Earth. The basic fact that the solar disc is barely covered by the Moon means that we can experience unprecedented views of the phenomena immediately above the solar photosphere (loosely speaking, the brilliant 'surface' of the Sun). The chromosphere, prominences and of course the corona, together with the processes taking place within these regions, were all discovered during total solar eclipses. Indeed, they are difficult to observe except during the 'perfect' total solar eclipses that we experience on Earth (although the inner chromosphere and large prominences can sometimes be glimpsed during deep annular eclipses, i.e., those falling barely short of totality).

Other than during solar eclipses, prominences may be observed by attaching a spectroscope to the eyepiece-end of a telescope and carefully aligning the latter until the limb of the photosphere becomes visible through the spectroscope's nearly-closed slit. The spectroscope is focused on one of the hydrogen lines in the solar spectrum and, if the slit is opened, any prominence within the (rather restricted) field of view will become visible. As a very small region of the solar limb is all that can be examined at any one time, this method is something of a hit-or-miss affair.

The solar corona has for years been studied by specially designed telescopes known as 'coronagraphs'. These, in effect, create artificial eclipses by obscuring the Sun with a disc within the telescope. The instrument was invented in the 1930s by Bernard Lyot, who employed it to observe the bright inner region of the corona, without the need for a total solar eclipse, from the exceptional site of the Pic du Midi Observatory in France. Further coronagraphs were subsequently constructed and sited at other high-altitude locations of exceptional atmospheric clarity. Although these instruments were deemed successful, observation was always difficult and the corona detail revealed fell short of that seen during eclipses. The biggest (one could really say, the *only*) advantage over eclipse observations was the convenience of being able to observe the corona whenever weather permitted and to extend these observations (once again, when weather permitted!) beyond the rather fleeting window of visibility offered by total solar eclipses. More recently, coronagraphs have been placed in outer space; a major leap forward occurring with the launch of three coronagraphs on board the Solar and Heliospheric Observatory (SOHO) in the mid 1990s. These have monitored the corona almost continuously at resolutions greater than anything possible from Earth, even during total solar eclipses.

Nevertheless, the invention of the coronagraph and its subsequent development into the likes of the instruments aboard SOHO, would probably not have happened had the corona not previously been observed during solar eclipses. There would have been little if any incentive to invent a coronagraph if nobody had any notion that such a thing as the corona existed. Would anyone have even considered blotting out the Sun if they had never experienced its natural occultation? Who would have bothered designing a special telescope for this purpose??

Similarly, although observing prominences by means of a spectroscope is not an especially difficult exercise, it is to be wondered whether anybody would have bothered had the existence of prominences not already been known from solar eclipse observations. Even if somebody had used a spectroscope to observe the limb of the Sun, would they have repeated the observation if no interesting features such as prominences had been in view?

Other stars also possess chromospheres, coronas and prominences, but they are all too remote to be directly observable. Nevertheless, because we can observe these phenomena directly in the Sun (thanks, in the first place, to the occurrence of perfect total solar eclipses) we are able to infer much about analogous phenomena in other stars, even in those that are quite dissimilar to our own Sun and display far more extreme analogues of solar phenomena. Spectral lines in the light of distant stars are provided with a benchmark for comparison thanks to observations of the phenomena associated with the Sun, and much can be learned that may otherwise have remained mysterious.

Even the most basic information about the Sun—and therefore about stars in general—came originally from observations of the chromosphere and prominences as seen against the dark backdrop of outer space; a view marvelously provided by perfect total solar eclipses. These observations demonstrated to astronomers of the mid Nineteenth Century that the Sun (and by implication, any star) is a huge ball of hot gas. Although this may seem obvious nowadays, to an earlier generation it constituted a fundamental discovery. We have already remarked how William Herschel, famed for his discovery of the planet Uranus, believed that what we perceive as the brilliant solar photosphere was really only the upper atmosphere of a gigantic planet-like body whose temperate surface supported an abundance of life. Even the discovery of the chromosphere by George Airy during the eclipse of July 28, 1851, was seriously misinterpreted.

Airy initially called the feature "the Sierra", erroneously thinking that he had found a range of gigantic mountains on the (presumably solid) surface of the Sun!

All such notions ended with the discovery of the gaseous spectrum of prominences by Pierre Jules Cesar Janssen during the eclipse of August 18, 1868. This observation—which led directly to Janssen's invention of a device known as the spectrohelioscope—proved the true nature of the Sun. The spectrohelioscope produces an image of the Sun in the light of a single spectral line, enabling astronomers to study motions within the solar atmosphere in great detail. Incidentally, this and allied spectroscopic work demolished Auguste Comte's pessimistic prophecy that the composition of the stars would forever remain a mystery to mankind!

Janssen's observations of the spectrum of prominences, as well as independent work in the same field by Joseph Norman Lockyer in England, led to the discovery of helium. Because this element has no absorption features in the solar spectrum, it could only be found by observing the emission spectrum of prominences. Thus, the discovery of the second most abundant element in the universe came directly from observations of prominences . . . which would themselves have been unknown except for the occurrence of perfect solar eclipses!

Another surprise awaited the astronomers of the latter decades of the Nineteenth Century. While observing the eclipse of December 22, 1870, astronomer Charles A. Young noticed that the Sun's spectrum suddenly switched from its usual appearance of sharp, dark, lines superimposed upon a bright continuous 'rainbow', to a series of bright lines. This only lasted for an instant, just as the total phase began. In other words, the spectrum changed from what astronomers call an absorption spectrum to an emission spectrum just at the onset of totality. An absorption spectrum occurs when the source of the continuum (the 'rainbow') is hotter than the surrounding gas through which its light passes. This is what we see in the 'normal' spectrum of the non-eclipsed Sun. However, the gas responsible for the absorption lines, even though cooler than the photosphere, is far from 'cool' by our everyday standards. Indeed, it would actually be seen as glowing if the greater light of the photosphere could be blocked out. This is in some respects analogous to the 'dark' sunspots that are observed on the photosphere. Although these appear dark when contrasted with their brilliant surroundings, they would actually be seen as brightly glowing if they could somehow be viewed against the black backdrop of space.

Young's observation revealed the source of the solar absorption spectrum to be confined to a thin layer within the chromosphere. During the brief period between the Moon's hiding of the photosphere and the obscuration of the narrow chromospheric region itself, the layer of gases responsible for the absorption spectrum became fleetingly visible against the background of outer space. Being so much hotter than empty space, the gaseous components of this layer were, for a brief instant, observed as glowing and therefore registered as an emission spectrum. In effect, the Moon itself acted as the slit of a giant natural spectroscope, permitting this so-called 'flash spectrum' to be observed and photographed. Thanks to this phenomenon, an interesting property of the Sun's lower 'atmosphere' was discovered.

Total solar eclipses also provided an early test—and confirmation—of the General Theory of Relativity. During totality, stars near the solar limb were photographed and their positions measured with high degree accuracy. These positions were then compared with accurate positional measurements secured months later at night. Both Einstein's theory and Newton's theory predict that rays of light bend in the presence of massive objects such as the Sun, and that there should in consequence be a small discrepancy between the positions secured during the eclipse and those secured at night. However, Einstein's theory predicted a measurably greater discrepancy than Newton's.

The critical experiment was performed during the eclipse of May 29, 1919, and the displacement found to agree with the predictions of Einstein's theory. This was quickly hailed as a spectacular confirmation of General Relativity.

Nevertheless, the effect remains a small one. For a displacement large enough to adequately test the two theories, stars being measured must lie almost in line with the solar limb. To secure this sufficient degree of accuracy therefore, the required eclipse must be total and at least nearly 'perfect' in the Gonzalez sense. Super eclipses hiding not just the Sun but also a significant region of surrounding space would make the experiment much more difficult. Hypothetical beings on Jupiter's moon Amalthea would not have been able to test General Relativity during any of *their* solar eclipses!

The extensive historical record of solar eclipses has also enabled us to trace changes in Earth's rotation period over the past few thousand years. The discovery that Earth's rotation is slowing (principally due to tides raised by the Moon and Sun) came about through careful measurement of stars, however the precision required for these observations has only been possible during the last couple of centuries. Needless to say, the rotational slowing is itself very slight; of the order of two milliseconds per day per century . . . hardly something that would readily be noticed by the casual observer!

Nevertheless, the effects of this rotational slowing actually do manifest in a way that can be observed. Because the path of totality of a solar eclipse is narrow, variations in the Earth's rotation period translate into errors in the path of the shadow track. By examining the times and places where eclipses occurred centuries ago and comparing these with the paths that the totality track would have taken had there been *no* alteration in the velocity of rotation, astronomers can measure the rate at which the Earth's rotation has changed. They have also been able to determine how the rate of slowing has varied over time. These variations are due to influences such as the retreat of glaciers in the Northern Hemisphere. Thus, data about variations in Earth's velocity of rotation indirectly provides information about these phenomena as well; information which opens an important window on climate changes over historically significant periods of time. In turn, this data may prove invaluable to the assessment of contemporary concerns such as global warming.

Because changes would be harder to discern if the tracks of totality were broad, perfect eclipses are also required for this information to be successfully gleaned from the ancient sources.

Records of ancient solar eclipses have also provided an important tool in the hands of historians, facilitating the translation of early calendar systems into our modern one. This has enabled them to construct a timeline of historical events.

It is also worth remarking that this long history of eclipse recording would probably not have eventuated had ancient peoples not reacted to these events with a very real sense of awe. To the ancients, these occurrences were more than natural curiosities and their careful recording of them reflects this fact. Even today, the drama and awe of seeing the Sun totally obscured by a blackened Moon as spectacular streamers of the corona flash into a deep twilight sky is a deeply moving experience where scientific thoughts are apt to become as eclipsed as the Sun itself. The author witnessed such an event in Turkey in 1999 and, at the moment of totality, the waiting crowd broke into spontaneous applause and cheering while a young child became terrified at the sudden onset of darkness. We moderns are not so very far removed from our ancestors when it comes to these types of happenings!

We shall return to the important subject of 'natural awe' later in this book

Measurability, habitability and the chemistry of life
Despite the fantasies of some science fiction writers and the wilder speculations of a few earlier scientists, most biologists nowadays believe that life cannot exist apart from carbon and water. Silicon salamanders wallowing in pools of liquid sulfur on Venus, ammonia-drinking, hydrogen-breathing, living dirigibles floating amid the clouds of Jupiter and some of the other wilder dreams of an earlier generation of exobiologists are now seen by most scientists as belonging with Hobbits and Orcs; only between the pages of a fantasy novel. They are almost certainly not denizens of the real universe.

Yet, it would seem at first glance that the most important chemicals of life (viz. carbon and water) should not exist on Earth at all. It is generally thought that the material from which our planet condensed was dry, much like the material found in ordinary stony meteorites. Water (mostly in the form of ice) and carbon compounds only appear in abundance in the Solar System at distances greater than about 400 million kilometers from the Sun, i.e. at least 2.5—3 times greater than Earth's distance. This region, the central and outer parts of the asteroid belt between the orbits of Mars and Jupiter, is predominantly populated by dark-colored asteroids rich in carbonaceous compounds and ice. The same general region is also the home of numerous short-period comets. Perhaps the chemical 'stuff of life' was transported to our planet in the form of carbon-and-water rich meteorites and impacting comets.

It was formerly thought that most of the water came from comets. This seemed to be a reasonable assumption, as these bodies are composed principally of ice. However, because the percentage of deuterium or 'heavy' hydrogen in cometary ice was shown to be significantly greater than that in terrestrial water, it now seems that at most 10% of our water could have originated from this source. Dark meteorites of the kind known as carbonaceous chondrites (thought to be pieces of the dark C-type asteroids that populate the asteroid belt at those distances where both water ice and carbon compounds begin to appear in abundance) are currently considered better candidates. The greater portion of carbon compounds may have been deposited by comets however, as these bodies are even more carbon-rich than the carbonaceous meteorites.

But where did our planet's store of those complex carbon compounds that we know as 'organic' originate?

In 1952, University of Chicago chemists Stanley Miller and Harold Urey discovered that organic molecules of a biologically interesting nature—namely amino acids and the amino acid chains called proteins—could be synthesized in the laboratory by passing electrical discharges through a gaseous mixture of hydrogen, water, ammonia and methane. At the time of the Miller-Urey experiment, this reducing gas mixture was thought to be representative of Earth's original atmosphere. The experiment was therefore hailed as a demonstration of how biologically significant organic molecules probably formed on the early Earth. Energetic processes such as lightning and ultraviolet solar radiation were hypothesized as having played analogous roles on early Earth as electric discharges in the laboratory experiment.

Later research cast doubt upon the applicability of this experiment to the early Earth, however, as models of the primordial atmosphere based upon the gases vented by present-day volcanic activity failed to yield the correct reducing mixture. Moreover, the very earliest rocks that have been preserved in the geologic record did not show any signs of having been exposed to a reducing atmosphere. On the contrary, they appeared to have formed in the presence of a neutral or even mildly oxidizing environment. This would not have been favorable to the Miller-Urey process. In view of this, the Miller-Urey process fell out of favour with most scientists as an explanation for terrestrial pre-biotic organic material and interest turned toward an extraterrestrial source such as carbonaceous asteroids and comets. These became increasingly seen as carriers, not just of simple carbon compounds, but of the very 'life chemicals' themselves.

There were very good reasons for suggesting such objects as the source of Earth's original store of organic materials. As we have already seen, the region of the Solar System beyond approximately 400 million kilometers of the Sun is a natural environment for both water ice and carbon compounds. Moreover, advances in the spectroscopic study of comets during the final decades of last century found the carbon compounds in these objects to be surprisingly complex and biologically interesting. Similarly, some very complex organic molecules, including amino acids, were found in carbonaceous meteorites. It therefore seemed a reasonable hypothesis that objects originating in these relatively remote regions of the planetary system should have supplied our planet with life-essential compounds

Although it became widely accepted, this hypothesis was not free of difficulties.

Principally, the way in which the required chemicals arrived on Earth seemed to limit the quantities that could have been transported in this way. That *some* organic compounds arrive from outer space is beyond dispute. We observe their arrival today in carbonaceous meteorites and cosmic dust. But the passage of a meteorite through our atmosphere is a very destructive process and there is no way of avoiding the conclusion that most organic material arriving from space is destroyed in its delivery. Could the surviving residual quantity have been sufficient to account for the rich organic endowment that our planet must have received prior to life's appearance?

There are signs that the tide of scientific opinion may yet turn back to the Miller-Urey process. Recent findings suggest that the classical objections to this process may be based upon some serious misconceptions about conditions on the early Earth.

First, there exists a growing body of evidence that the very earliest terrestrial epoch, the so-called 'Hadean' age (a word derived from 'Hades'), may have been less 'hellish' than originally thought. Although no rocks dating from this period have been unearthed, crystals of zircon recovered in Western Australia are estimated to have formed at least 4.2 billion years ago—long predating the rocks in which they were found. This places their time of formation within the Hadean era. Isotopes of oxygen trapped within these tiny crystals can yield significant information about conditions existing at the time of their crystallization. Because the ratios of these isotopes are sensitive to the presence of water and temperatures existing at that time, these factors can be deduced from the measured ratio. Surprisingly, analysis of the oxygen isotope ratio yielded results that could only be explained by the existence of liquid water and relatively cool surface temperatures at the time the zircons formed.[2] This evidence of a cool and wet environment strongly conflicts with the traditional picture of Hadean times.

If this evidence is verified, the possibility is at least open that the neutral/weakly oxidizing atmosphere to which the earliest surviving rocks had been exposed was not the most primitive that Earth possessed. Absence of evidence for a reducing atmosphere would no longer equate to evidence for the absence of such an early gaseous mantel. It also opens the possibility that organic material may have accumulated on the Earth, and in ancient seas, hundreds of millions of years earlier than hitherto believed and even that microbial life could have appeared much earlier than has been generally accepted.[3]

Of even greater possible significance however, is the research of Bruce Fegley and Laura Schaefer[4] into the types of gases likely to have been vented by early volcanic activity. A major objection to the development of an early reducing atmosphere concerned the composition of the gas mixture vented by modern volcanoes. This mixture could not yield the right type of atmosphere for the Miller-Urey process to work. Assuming that primordial volcanoes vented essentially the same mixture of gases as their modern counterparts, it was concluded that Earth could not have acquired an atmosphere in which the process could get under way.

Although this appeared a reasonable line of argument, Fegley and Schaefer found that by heating meteorites of the ordinary chondrite variety—believed to be remnants of the material from which the terrestrial planets formed—a gaseous mix evolved that was markedly different from that vented by contemporary volcanoes. Specifically, it possessed a significantly higher proportion of reducing gases. If this mixture was representative of early terrestrial out gassing, the Earth's first atmospheric mantel would have been strongly reducing; exactly as required for the Miller-Urey process to proceed!

Whether these findings stand up to examination remains to be seen, so we cannot yet be sure as to whether the Miller-Urey process will be, as it were, rehabilitated. Nevertheless, at the moment it is starting to look as if its demise may have been, in Mark Twain's words, "greatly exaggerated".

Even if this is upheld however, it does not necessarily mean that the organic contribution from comets and asteroidal meteorites can be discounted. As so often happens, the truth may not be 'either/or' so much as 'both'. The Earth's early store of organic material must have been great and it would not be surprising if both sources turned out to be vital.

It is even possible that an important source of extraterrestrial material has been overlooked. Since the launch of the solar-observing SOHO spacecraft in the mid 1990s, an almost constant stream of tiny comets has been observed approaching the Sun to within very small distances. Most of these belong to a 'group' of so-called 'sungrazing' comets which had been known for many years before the launch of SOHO, and which actually includes some of the most brilliant comets on record. Minor members of the group had previously been observed by an earlier generation of orbital solar observatories in the late 1970s and 1980s, so the existence per se of these minor comets was not too surprising. What did come as a surprise was the huge number and extremely small dimensions of the majority of objects recorded.

An even bigger surprise was the discovery that SOHO data included many equally tiny comets (most of them not recognized in initial assessments of the data) that did not belong to this group. Until then, the 'sungrazers' tended to be considered as anomalies . . . fragments of a comet that ventured freakishly close to the Sun in times past and fragmented into myriads of pieces; some large, but the majority very tiny. The new discoveries, however, showed that this group was not alone in undergoing multiple disruption processes. Not only do tiny comets exist that were not members of the group, but some of these were also marshaled into *different* groups. Until the SOHO data was analyzed, no other comet group had been found.

Some of these objects were truly tiny; in the order of just ten meters (compared with diameters ranging from about one to thirty kilometers or larger for 'regular' comets). Several astronomers independently noticed that the mean orbit of one of these newly discovered groups implied that its members could pass very close to Earth if the time of their passage happened to fall within very narrow time constraints. Amazingly, one object found in archived SOHO data recorded in 1999 had indeed made such a close passage of our planet. According to the best calculated orbit, this object came closer than any other recorded comet, yet at the time nobody knew anything about it! The comet was not actually discovered until a couple of years later, following the launch of a systematic search for small comets in archived SOHO images.

A very close similarity between this potentially Earth-approaching group of comets and a well-known annual meteor shower was first pointed out by the present author[5] and an association between both and a known comet (96P/Machholz) that returns every five years was found by Brian Marsden of the Centre for Astronomical Telegrams. Dr. Marsden, incidentally, was also the first to recognize the existence of this particular comet group.

Tiny objects of this nature could hit the Earth and probably not even be noticed. It has been suggested informally that they might disrupt high in the atmosphere without the appearance of a meteoric fireball. If this is true, organic-rich cometary material could be deposited into our upper atmosphere and inconspicuously filter down to the surface with little disruption.

Moreover, very small comets are apparently not confined to these 'sungrazing' and 'sunskirting' varieties. On September 26, 2004, astronomer M. E. Van Ness found a faint comet that, according to calculations by Professor Z. Sekanina, et al[6] had a nucleus a mere four *meters* in diameter. In comparison with the 'text-book' comets—mostly between one and ten *kilometers* in diameter—not to mention the occasional giant such as Hale-Bopp (probably about fifty kilometers across), we can appreciate how tiny Van Ness' comet really was. Not surprisingly, this object broke up and disappeared within a month of discovery. Had it been on a collision course with Earth, this debris cloud, presumably well endowed with organic molecules, may simply have sifted through our atmosphere unnoticed by anyone. Actually, this comet was moving in an orbit that prevented it from hitting the Earth, but over the course of time, especially in the Solar System's youth, many similar objects must have hit our planet.

In May 2006, Earth experienced the unusually close approach of a small comet known as 73P/Schwassmann-Wachmann. This event was made especially unusual by the fact that the comet had suffered a partial disruption during a previous passage (actually two passages, or eleven years, earlier) and in 2006 appeared at the head of a train of scores of fragments, strung like beads across millions of kilometers of space. These, in effect, had become little comets in their own right. A spectacular series of images of the brightest member of this stream of secondary comets, obtained by the Hubble Space Telescope, revealed that it was also disrupting and shedding scores of mini-minicomets down its tail. Had Earth passed through the tail, we would surely have picked up a quantity of organic material as these objects disrupted in our atmosphere. There was actually no possibility of any of these fragments hitting Earth, nor was it possible for a passage through the brighter fragment's tail, but similar events must have happened innumerable times during the history of our globe and countless hits undoubtedly scored over the ages.

From early 1972 until late 1974, the artificial satellite HEOS-2 monitored cosmic dust in the Earth's immediate space environment and during this period recorded several occasions when the number of dust impacts on the satellite soared far beyond the normal frequency. The only explanation seemed to be the passage of HEOS through clouds of dust in near-Earth space. It is thought that these clouds resulted from the total disruption of low density objects, presumably of cometary origin, as they passed close to Earth. A very fragile body passing through the Earth's auroral zones will build up an electrostatic charge on its surface and, if the repellent force of the charge exceeds the tensile strength of the object, disrupt totally. From the amount of dust observed in these clouds, initial masses of the bodies concerned were estimated to have ranged from around 100 grams to about one ton.[7] The larger ones may have been similar to the tiny comets in the tail of the brighter Schwassmann-Wachmann secondary. Presumably, organic molecules were mixed with the dust of these clouds, and it is interesting to note how the existence of auroral zones, and the terrestrial magnetic field responsible for these, may therefore have played a role in the capture of at least some cometary organics.

In short, the organic stock of the early Earth may have consisted of material arriving from comets and dark carbonaceous asteroids *and* from the synthesis —via the Miller-Urey process—of reducing gases derived from the heating of ordinary chondritic material from which the planet initially accreted. Both may have been equally important to the subsequent history of our planet.

What ever the source of Earth's initial stock of organic compounds, its continuing supply depended from an early time upon synthesis by simple living organisms. These appeared very early in the life of our planet and the process of life itself constitutes the most efficient mechanism for synthesizing carbon compounds.

Simple, early, life gave Earth its oxygen atmosphere, in turn enabling more complex forms to exist and thrive. Marine organisms deposit carbon compounds on the ocean floor; deposits which are gradually recycled through deeper regions of the Earth as the ocean plates subduct via plate tectonics. This carbon is eventually recycled back into the atmosphere through volcanic vents in the form of carbon dioxide. This process—the carbon cycle—plays an essential role in regulating Earth's temperature, as we saw in Chapter One.

Water is just as important for life as carbon. An abundance of water drives the hydrological cycle, in turn giving rise to the process of sedimentation. Layer upon layer of sediment, deposited on the floors of lakes and oceans, eventually compresses into rock in which the fossil records of previous ages become preserved, a little like the pressed flowers that grandma kept between the pages of thick books.

In addition, the accumulation of ice sheets records climatic and biological changes extending over many thousands of years. It even gives us a means of determining what our planet's atmosphere was like in past millennia. Tiny bubbles of air trapped within the ice provide us with well-preserved samples of ancient air which scientists can now analyze in their laboratories. The hydrological cycle, in addition to maintaining a habitable environment, has transformed the planet into a great library of ancient scientific data.

Yet, even given a hydrological cycle, these repositories of data are not necessarily guaranteed. The Earth's hydrological cycle strikes a happy mean between having so little water that deposited sediments would become readily exposed and any data contained within them destroyed (or at least strongly degraded) by erosion and so much water that dry land areas would be few and far between and sediments produced by erosion too diffused within the vast oceans. Likewise, too little land would not be conducive to the building up of the vast ice sheets that have provided such treasures of ancient data.

Too little water would also be bad news for the carbon cycle. We recall from our discussion in Chapter One how insufficient water results in a seizing up of the plate tectonic mechanism. Without the plate tectonic engine to disperse internal planetary heat, volcanism increases and the atmosphere becomes overloaded with greenhouse gases. The more rapid recycling of Earth's crust through this enhanced volcanic activity would also destroy geologically stored information on a shorter timescale. However, as this volcanic Earth is unlikely to be habitable, this probably has little practical consequence!

It appears, therefore, that a significantly greater or smaller quantity of water on the Earth would result in *both* an environment more hostile to complex life *and* an environment less friendly to the storing of information about the planet's past.

Furthermore, as Gonzalez and Richards remark,[8] it is surely surprising that terrestrial processes should encode such high-grade information as a mere by-product of cosmic evolution. It is also noteworthy that this information confers no survival advantage on terrestrial biology and was not even accessible to life until very recent times.

Earthquakes and magnetic fields

Most earthquakes occur as by-products of plate tectonics. In view of the terrible destruction often caused by earthquakes and their siblings, tsunami, we may be excused for not always seeing plate tectonics in as positive a light as presented here!

Nevertheless, the benefits of the process outweigh its detriments.

Ward and Brownlee sum up the importance of plate tectonics with respect to terrestrial life in the following words;

> Plate tectonics plays at least three crucial roles in maintaining animal life. It promotes biological productivity; it promotes diversity (the hedge against mass extinction); and it helps maintain equable temperatures, a necessary requirement for animal life. It may be that plate tectonics is the central requirement for life on a planet and that it is necessary for keeping a world supplied with water.[9]

Therefore, even if earthquakes per se may not be especially beneficial for life on this planet, they represent the inevitable consequences of a process which is not merely beneficial to life, but *absolutely essential for its existence.*

Yet, even if earthquakes may not be beneficial to life in general, they *are* of great benefit to those living organisms whose chosen work is to learn more about the interior workings of our planet; those intelligent organisms called geophysicists! Every strong earthquake sets waves radiating throughout the globe of the Earth, eventually reaching every region of our planet. If seismographs are well distributed across the Earth's surface, their recordings of these vibrations (too minute to be detected without instruments, except for those living relatively close to the earthquake's epicenter) enable geophysicists to build up a three-dimensional profile of the planet's interior. In the words of Gonzalez and Richards, this technique (known technically as three-dimensional tomography) provides what is in essence a geological CAT scan.

In another remarkable 'coincidence', the epoch of Earth's history that saw the appearance of geophysicists and their seismographs also happens to be the epoch when these instruments can most effectively be used to map the interior of Earth. Two hundred million years ago (not a long time geologically speaking) the Earth possessed a single continent called Pangaea. The rest of our world was a great ocean. This super continent has since broken up and its pieces —the continental land masses of today—scattered across the once watery face of the globe. Amongst other benefits, this diffusion of land masses allowed a global distribution of seismic observatories, and it is this that makes detailed charting of the planet's interior possible. Had a united Pangaea been the home of the human race, much less would have been learned about the interior of our globe.

The study of earthquakes and other geophysical phenomena enables geophysicists to acquire a great deal of information about the properties of the Earth's outer core. They have deduced, for instance, that it is composed of iron at temperatures that may well be as high as 3,000 degrees Celsius. Heat flowing through this outer core causes it to convect and, being a conductor of electricity, sets up a dynamo generator. Unlike man-made dynamos employing permanent magnets, the geo-dynamo must regenerate its own magnetic field. This is in part generated and maintained by the planet rotating fast enough to produce eddies in the outer core.

The geo-dynamo is responsible for Earth's magnetic field; a field which plays such a vital role in shielding the surface of the planet, and the living organisms inhabiting it, from damaging cosmic radiation.

The magnetic field leaves records of itself by determining the alignment of ferromagnetic materials as they sink to form undisturbed marine sediments. Moreover, it also leaves behind its record by becoming 'frozen' in basaltic lava which has cooled below the so-called Curie point; the temperature above which rock loses its magnetism. Studies of this frozen field in lava flows provide geophysicists with a record of changes and reversals in the terrestrial magnetic field over many hundreds of thousands of years.

In the late 1950s, ships trailing magnetometers carried out extensive mapping of ancient magnetic fields preserved in the rocks of the ocean floor. This project resulted in a fascinating and unexpected discovery. The resultant maps were found to display a pattern of magnetic polarity reversals running parallel to the mid-ocean ridges and symmetrically placed on both sides of these ridges. These strips, it was subsequently discovered, resulted from reversals of the Earth's magnetic field. As fresh sea floor crust formed and spread out on both sides of the ridge, the patterns of these magnetic reversals became frozen into the crustal material. This process effectively turned the ocean floor into a gigantic magnetic tape recorder!

For this to have occurred, however, a rather incredible degree of fine tuning of the reversal rate of the Earth's magnetic field, the spreading rate of the ocean floor, the depth of the ocean and the temperatures of the Earth was required. As geophysicist David Sandwell writes in his book *Plate Tectonics: An Insider's History of the Modern Theory of the Earth*;

> Most of this magnetic field is recorded in the upper mile or two of the oceanic crust. If the thickness of this layer were too great, then as the plate cooled as it moved off the spreading ridge axis, the positive and negative reversals would be juxtaposed in dipping layers; this superposition would smear the pattern observed by a ship. On Earth, the temperatures are just right for creating a thin magnetized layer.[10]

Furthermore, these remnant field variations must be viewed at the right distance if they are to be read by means of ship-born magnetometers. They would appear to simply 'smooth out' if viewed from too far away. If a signal is to remain strong at the ocean surface, the spacing of the magnetic strips needs to be about 6.3 times the ocean depth.

Sandwell continues;

> Half-spreading rates on Earth vary from 6 to 50 miles (10 to 80 kilometres) per million years. This suggests that for the magnetic anomalies to be most visible on the ocean surface, the reversal rate should be between 2.5 and 0.3 million years. It is astonishing that this is the typical reversal rate observed in sequences of lava flows on land . . . This lucky convergence of length and timescales *makes it very unlikely that magnetic anomalies, due to crustal spreading, will ever be observed on another planet*[11]. (My emphasis).

It is amazing indeed that information coding a detailed history of the ocean floor has been recorded in a way that can be relatively easily accessed by a technological civilization. It is even more remarkable that the rare planet (maybe the *only* planet as Sandwell opines) possessing conditions that enable this to occur also happens to be the one (once again, maybe the only one) enjoying conditions favoring its habitation by just such a technological civilization!

It is equally remarkable, that there should be such a dramatic overlap of the factors enabling Earth to possess the remarkable information-storing abilities of which we have been speaking and conditions suitable for the existence of creatures benefiting from this feature. Central to both are; a supply of water sufficient to yield deep oceans (but not so much water as to flood the entire planet to great depths), a magnetic field that deflects cosmic radiation harmful to complex life and a continuing plate tectonic mechanism. Once again, there is no *a priori* reason why the mechanisms enabling habitability should also be those ensuring intelligibility. We may simply take this for granted, but its familiarity occults a profound philosophical mystery that is only made intelligible if, somehow, this 'co-incidence' has been *planned* to happen. We shall return to this point later.

Sundry interesting 'coincidences'

We will only quickly mention the other aspects of the habitability/intelligibility correspondence examined by Gonzalez and Richards in their book. For further information we again direct the reader to their work, remembering however that even their research is preliminary and undoubtedly only scratches the surface of this vast topic.

On a quick tour through the topic, we note first the transparent atmosphere of Earth. Necessary for the rays of the Sun to reach the surface with sufficient intensity to sustain life, our atmosphere nevertheless offers a degree of protection not present in the very thin and highly transparent atmosphere of Mars, whose surface is exposed to the full intensity of sterilizing ultraviolet radiation. Yet our atmosphere is sufficiently thin and transparent to permit observation of the remoter parts of the universe. Imagine, if we can, intelligent beings inhabiting the surface of Venus. How, we wonder, would their view of the universe and their place within it have evolved beneath their perpetually clouded skies?

The transparency of our atmosphere may also have a decidedly practical advantage to life on Earth, but one which we are only now reaching the stage of technological sophistication to exploit. We refer to the ability (certainly denied our imaginary friends on Venus!) to image faint Solar System objects such as small asteroids and comets that may collide with our planet at some time in the future. The consequences of an impact by the larger objects of these classes would be horrendous for all life on Earth. Even the impact by a small asteroid, such as the one which struck the Tunguska region of Siberia in 1908, has the potential to wipe out a city. Had the 1908 object arrived just a few hours later, it would have blasted right into St. Petersburg!

Several comets and many asteroids are discovered each year. Some of the comets have periods of revolution of many thousands of years, but few of these come too close to Earth and although the occasional one must hit on timescales of millions of years, the probability of any one hitting on any particular return is very slight. Of greater potential danger are the asteroids which cross Earth's orbit, and comets of short period (less than ten years or thereabouts) which are often a lot less active than their long-period relatives and therefore fainter and harder to detect. Their faintness does not, however, necessarily reflect smaller size, just weaker activity. Moreover, their orbits are constantly being altered by the gravitational influence of Jupiter and ones that came nowhere near Earth fifty years ago may now be in orbits that are potentially hazardous. Chances are, if we ever discover an asteroid or comet that is destined to strike, it will not be during the discovery loop of its orbit. The danger will more likely become apparent when the orbit of the object is projected into the future and it is found to occupy the same position as Earth in, say, thirty or fifty years time. That should give us time for a response to be worked out and a major disaster hopefully avoided.

Earlier, we saw how the diameter of Earth's orbit around the Sun is critical for the maintenance of life-supporting conditions on this planet. But the diameter of our planet's orbit has another beneficial function as well. It enables astronomers to measure the distance of the nearer stars!

Hold a pencil at arm's length and close your left eye. Line up the image of the pencil against a more distant object a door handle or a tree in the neighbor's garden for instance. Now close your left eye and open the right. The pencil no longer lines up with the distant object. This is a homely example of parallax and if you know the exact distance between the pupils of your eyes, a little math will enable you to calculate the distance of the pencil and, therefore, the length of your arm.

Similarly, if an astronomer measures the exact position of a 'nearby' star (relative to the remote background ones) and then, six months later when the Earth is on the exact other side of its orbit, measures it again, the two positions should not quite agree, just as the two positions of the pencil did not agree when viewed from alternate eyes. Knowing the diameter of Earth's orbit, the astronomer can readily calculate the distance of the star.

It will be readily appreciated that if our orbit had been smaller, the distance for which this parallax method remained effective would be correspondingly reduced and the numbers of stars available for measure considerably fewer. We also note that had the Sun been cooler, the Earth's orbit would need to have been reduced if habitable temperatures were to be maintained (but then, our closer proximity to the 'Sun' would have made us more vulnerable to energetic particles from flares. Fainter stars, paradoxically, have more vigorous flares).

A smaller orbit, with its smaller parallax, would decrease the chances of astronomers having within reach of direct measurement, the rare but very brilliant O and B type stars. Fortunately, a few of these giants have had their distances measured by the parallax method; something which would not have been possible had Earth been located in, say, Mercury's orbit. The value of directly measuring the distances of stars of this class is related to their well determined luminosity. Once the distances of a few are found by the parallax method, a comparison of their apparent brightness with that of more remote stars of the same class readily enables the distances of the latter to be calculated . Because these stars have such a great real or 'absolute' brightness, they can be seen in far regions of the Galaxy and therefore make very efficient standard candles for determining the distances of remote stellar clusters.

Had Earth's orbit been larger, a greater parallax would have meant more accessible stars, but this would have come at a price. Larger orbits mean longer times between measurements. Rather than waiting six months between making the precise measurements of stars to obtain a parallax, hypothetical astronomers on Jupiter would be required to wait almost six *years*. Earth's orbit provides a good compromise between the time taken to acquire the requisite observations and the number of stars within range of parallax measurement.

Thus, the radius of Earth's orbit around the Sun, in addition to being just right for the existence of advanced life, also appears to be just right for providing ways in which the most inquisitive example of this life can satisfy its curiosity concerning the size of its cosmic environment. But it is also true that the Sun's (or, rather, the Solar System's) orbit around the centre of the Milky Way galaxy is equally beneficial in both these respects. We will look at this shortly, but first let us set the scene with a brief overview of the universe of galaxies.

Any view of the universe that encompasses truly cosmic distances, such as the deep field images taken by the Hubble Space Telescope, easily reveals the basic 'building blocks' of the universe to be galaxies rather than individual stars. A long exposure image of deep space taken through a large telescope typically shows a smattering of faint stars, all of which are 'local' in the sense of belonging to our own galaxy, and a number of objects that look like star images seen slightly out of focus. One or two of these may appear large enough to take on a definite shape, either a featureless fuzzy blob not unlike a luminous cotton wool ball or a tight swirl that might remind one of a dab of cream swirling in a vigorously stirred cup of coffee. Other, less regular, shapes may be represented as well. How many of these objects appear in the image depends upon how large the telescope is and how long the exposure has taken. Larger telescopes and longer exposure times (other things being equal) record fainter objects and, as the fainter outnumber the brighter, more and more of these objects will be revealed until we reach something like the very deep exposures of Hubble, which are simply crowded with very faint fuzzy star-like images.

They may look tiny and faint, but each of these objects is really a vast system of stars. These are the "galaxies". The word is derived from "milk" and describes the milky appearance of brighter members of the class as observed visually at the eyepiece of a telescope. We recall that our Sun, together with Earth and the rest of the Solar System, is located within one of these galaxies, usually called the Milky Way or simply, the Galaxy. The Sun is, as we saw earlier, just one of an estimated three or four billion stars comprising the Galaxy, together with vast clouds of matter from which new stars are continually forming and into which old dying stars leave part of their remains in the form of gas and dust enriched by elements synthesized in the thermonuclear inferno that once burnt within their cores.

The Milky Way is a spiral galaxy. That is to say, it is one of those with the 'cream in the coffee' swirl or, if you prefer, the shape of a nautilus shell. Measuring over sixty light years across it is, however, an unusually large spiral galaxy. The Sun orbits in a remarkably low-eccentricity orbit about 24,000 light years from the Galaxy's centre (remembering that a light year is the *distance*—it is not a measure of time—that light travels in a year at the velocity of around 300,000 kilometers per *second*).

Beyond our own Galaxy, thousands of millions of other galaxies—each a vast system of millions or billions of stars—fade off into the cosmic distance.

We already saw in the first chapter how the Sun's location within the Milky Way, with respect to its location not too close to the dense and dangerous heartland yet not so far out in the fringes as to be starved of heavy elements, determines it's potential for possessing a habitable planet. We also saw how its orbit close to the mid plane of the galaxy probably helps protect terrestrial life from the radiation of energetic events within the body of the Galaxy. At present, the Solar System is very close to the galactic mid plane, having crossed through it only three to five million years ago . . . a mere 'yesterday' in cosmic terms.

We also noted that the Solar System is located between two of the major arms of the Galaxy, thus ensuring that we are relatively safe from nearby supernova and gravitational disturbances of the Sun's comet cloud through close passages of giant molecular clouds or large clusters of stars.

But our location between major spiral arms, in addition to helping maintain our continued existence, also provides us with a relatively clear view of deep space. Our location away from the galactic heartland likewise helps in this respect and even our location very close to the galactic mid plane, rather surprisingly, does not diminish this clear view. The region of space in which the Solar System lies appears to be starved of gas and dust in comparison with most of the local galactic mid plane!

When we consider the universe at large, a great deal has been written in recent years about the exquisite fine tuning of the various parameters required to make the universe habitable. But Gonzalez and Richards note that this same fine tuning also renders the universe intelligible to any sufficiently intelligent life form within it. They write;

> The striking capacity of the cosmos for discovery also depends on the particular forms of the laws and values of the physical constants ... [this is] astonishingly pervasive, even at the very foundations of matter. For example, the existence of discrete energy states at the quantum level permits astronomers to extract detailed information from light emitting bodies with spectroscopic analysis. Atomic regularity results in a distinctive spectroscopic signature of each element and molecule.... The astronomer E. A. Milne once noted that if the laws of nature had produced a nonquantum microscopic realm characterized by continuous energy distributions ... spectroscopy would have been a far less useful tool.[12]

In similar vein, these authors also point out that even the very basic fact that each fundamental particle has a universal mass greatly enhances scientific measurement by ensuring that the conclusions reached through experiments conducted in laboratories on Earth are equally applicable to objects at the furthest reaches of the universe. They continue,

> Since the existence of the elements, and hence life, depends on distinct quantum states and the mass constancy of fundamental particles, habitability and measurability are yoked, it seems, all the way down.[13]

Although a lot more could be said about this matter of habitability and discoverability, the above should be sufficient to define the main thrust of the argument. This is neatly summed up in the words of Gonzalez and Richards, viz.

> The myriad conditions that make a region [of the universe] habitable are also the ones that make the best overall places for discovering the universe in its smallest and largest expressions.[14]

How significant though, is this correlation? Might it simply be that because the conditions for habitability are so complex and (it increasingly appears) so rare that the conditions suitable for discoverability (which, we might reasonably suppose to be complex as well) become more likely? Does the argument simply demonstrate that it is complexity itself that makes an environment both habitable and measurable?

Gonzalez and Richards, while allowing some superficial plausibility to this position, argue that it ultimately fails a deeper examination. Complexity per se, implies neither habitability nor discoverability. For example, the cloudy chaotic atmosphere of Jupiter is no less complex than that of Earth, yet, it is far less habitable. We may add that even if intelligent beings could somehow manage to survive within its murky depths, they would also find it a great hindrance to discovering anything of the universe beyond their gargantuan orb.

Conversely, there is nothing especially complex about perfect solar eclipses. The deep solar eclipses observable from Jupiter's moon Amalthea are no less complex than the ones observed from Earth; nevertheless, they are far less capable of yielding fundamental facts about the universe.

The possession of complexity per se seems less significant than it might have done at first glance. The significant point is not that habitability and discoverability each possess complexity but, rather, that they each share in an over-reaching *transitive* complexity.

In other words, the fine tunings, knife-edge balances and highly improbably convergences of many factors that together enable this little niche of the universe to be habitable, are in themselves suggestive of transitivity. Yet the case is not so tight as to be immediately compelling. They appear to point toward life, but a skeptic may still object that this is simply an argument after the fact. The 'fact' is that life exists, and that it requires a very fine balance to be maintained. This (the skeptics say) does not require a "Why?" . . . it is simply a fact of existence. It should not be surprising that a phenomenon as complex as life should require an extremely precise set of conditions for its occurrence. We observe the fine tuning simply because we would not be here to find anything at all if the fine tuning did not exist.

We have already commented critically on this line of argument, but we will allow it to stand for the present. However, it clearly fails to explain the fine tuning evidenced in discoverability. Even if we were to grant that an environment suitable for life must give the appearance of having been fined tuned, it does not follow that an environment suitable for discovery must have a similar appearance. Our existence does not depend upon our ability to discover facts about the universe, nor is there any *a priori* reason why a potentially habitable zone must also be a suitable region from which discoveries can readily be made. Specifically, there is no *necessary* connection between our presence on this planet and its exquisite suitability as a platform for discovery. There is a logical reason for maintaining that we would not be here if conditions were not conducive to habitability, but there is no logical reason for arguing that we would not be here if conditions were not conducive to discoverability. Neither is there a logical reason for arguing that the same conditions suitable for habitability must also be suitable for discoverability. It is not *logically* impossible that the most suitable place for intelligent life should lie deep within the opaque atmosphere of Jupiter. That this is factually incorrect *given the physical laws of our universe* is not an objection. *It is the very crux of the issue.*

Why should the conditions of habitability just happen to coincide with the conditions of discoverability?

Why should the physical laws of the universe be such as to bring this coincidence about?

Why should we be living in a universe where these laws govern reality?

Why should the universe have come together in such a way as to yield this result?

To these questions we add yet another:

Why did nature bring forth, as the most complex life form in the habitable environment, a creature with what could only be called an excess of cosmic curiosity?

Let us elaborate on what we mean by "cosmic curiosity". We may recall that we, earlier, used the phrase "biological luxury" to describe the sort of desires and psychological characteristics that do not seem necessary for biological survival, but which nevertheless add to the, so to speak, 'humanness' of life. Curiosity, at its most basic and practical level is not a biological luxury. Being curious about which berries are edible and which are poisonous, which animals have a taste for human flesh and so forth certainly has survival value. It is also very practical to know which plant leaves can be used to soothe painful skin diseases and to discover which twigs give a scented smoke capable of driving away mosquitoes. But the urge to measure the distance of the Andromeda galaxy, or the desire to build particle accelerators capable of discovering the composition of an atomic nucleus hardly seems necessary for survival. Likewise, there seems little survival value in philosophizing about the nature of universal terms or the fate of time if space were to shrink to a geometric point.

Yet, these types of questions have exercised the brightest of human minds since at least the time of Thales of Miletos.

Questions of this nature have also driven men and women to spend billions of dollars on telescopes and particle accelerators and other instruments of pure research. There are those in our society who decry this 'waste of resources', but there are many more who see it not as a waste, but as money well spent on the fulfillment of a very basic human desire. But why are we so driven to spend large sums of money on pure research? Or, on a smaller scale, why is a keen amateur astronomer willing to spend a goodly portion of his annual income on the purchase of a new telescope?

One may answer that such pure research is of value in improving the intellectual quality of life. But this is restating the question rather than answering it. It assumes that the acquisition of such knowledge is self-evidently a good pursuit. But the real issue is *why* we intuitively feel that it is a good and worthy pursuit. Cats and dogs, monkeys and whales apparently get along quite well without it, so why can't we?

Why do we feel—why is it so self evidently true—that we would lack something vital if we ceased these pursuits?

Some 'pure research' speculations *have* recently emerged as having potential survival value, but thousands of years too late for this fact to offer an explanation in Darwinian terms.

For example, curiosity about the nature of the atom led to the use of radiation as a means of treating cancer (it also led to the atomic bomb, which does *not* have survival value!) and even more recently, the charting of asteroids and comets that regularly visit the inner Solar System on short-period orbits has led to a better assessment of the chances of a devastating impact which, in turn, is starting to bring forth plans as to how any such foreseen event may be avoided. This might yet have immense survival value, but the capacity to engage in the type of research required and the curiosity to contemplate even the possibility of such can hardly be explained in terms of natural selection favoring these traits.

It is the curiosity about these more fundamental matters—this, in a manner of speaking, *abstract* curiosity that is not obviously associated with biological survival—that we choose to term "cosmic curiosity".

On the face of it, there would seem to be no reason as to why nature should have (a) selected in favour of beings possessing cosmic curiosity and (b) been so benign as to make the extremely narrow set of conditions under which they could survive coextensive with the set enabling them to satisfy this cosmic curiosity.

One may argue that certain aspects of Earth's environment are suitable for the encouragement of cosmic curiosity. For example, the clear atmosphere enables views of distant worlds. Over the centuries this has encouraged speculation as to what these worlds might be. Thunder and lightning and other awesome phenomena have also exercised human imagination and curiosity. But these phenomena, though they may encourage an already-existing cosmic curiosity, could not generate it. A young child asks "Why?" in connection with all manner of things, but a cat, whose intelligence is said to equal that of a two-year-old and which is traditionally known as a curious animal, takes no notice of anything not impinging upon its own food and comfort.

Why should a purely mechanical nature—a blind watchmaker, so to speak —just happen to be so benevolent?

Why should nature "red in tooth and claw" be concerned only to endow us with those desires capable of satiation in a habitable environment?

Richard Dawkins writes, "The universe we observe has precisely the properties we should expect if there is at bottom no design, no purpose, no evil, no good, nothing but blind, pitiless indifference."[15] This is simply not correct. The very fact that "the universe we observe" is observable at all betrays the presence of a curious beneficence. How ever one might attempt to explain this, it remains an empirical fact or, to be more precise, it remains the pre-condition for our knowledge of a wide range of empirical facts.

What are the chances that a random convergence of factors should give rise to an environment simultaneously allowing, *both*, the existence of a class of organism possessing the 'biological luxury' of cosmic curiosity *and* the satiation of this curiosity?

We can find no answer to this question. Indeed, we find it incredibly unlikely that such a link between cosmic curiosity and our existence in an environment find-tuned for discovery should exist at all. That such a situation, with all the appearance of purposeful planning, could have arisen simply by the interplay of blind chance stretches credibility. Blind chance can no more account for this than for the painted arrow on a parking lot floor. Like this latter, the habitability/discoverability conjunction is an instance of TC. Both habitability and discoverability converge to establish a niche for a being possessed of cosmic curiosity. Moreover, we note that this apparent purpose is fulfilled by the fact that just such a being occupies this niche; a being displaying the appearance of having been specially crafted for this very environment, not just as a survivor (as natural selection might have decreed) but as one who fulfils his cosmic curiosity by using this special place as a remarkably efficient platform of discovery. Just as the painted arrow was revealed as being transitive by actually fulfilling the function for which it appeared to have been made, so habitability and discoverability, together in tandem, reveal an analogous transitivity by actually producing the state of affairs for which they appear to have been so carefully coordinated.

As with the arrow, so here, the only rational conclusion is that some form of intelligence is involved. Here, however, the intelligence must be of truly cosmic proportions.

Notes

1. Guillermo Gonzalez and Jay Richards, *The Privileged Planet: How Our Place in the Cosmos is Designed for Discovery* (Washington DC: Regnery Publishing, 2004), 334.
2. John W. Valley, "A Cool Early Earth," Scientific American 293 (October 2005): 40-47.
3. Eugenie Samuel Reich, "What the hell ...?" New Scientist 186 (14 May 205): 41-43.
4. Tony Fitzpatrick, "Calculations Favour Reducing Atmosphere of Early Earth: Was the Miller-Urey Experiment Correct?" Public release of finding presented at annual meeting of the Division of Planetary Sciences of the American Astronomical Society, Sept. 4-9, 2005.
5. Brian Marsden, Minor Planets Electronic Circular 2002 - E25.
6. Zdenek Sekanina, Milos Tichy, Jana Tisha and Michal Kocer, "C/2004 S1 (van Ness): A Split, Suddenly Vanishing Comet," International Comet Quarterly 27 (July 2005): 141-156.
7. H. Fechtig, "Cometary Dust in the Solar System: II Dust Swarms," Comets, Laurel L. Wilkening (ed.) (Tucson Arizona: The University of Arizona Press, 1982), 373-376.
8. Gonzalez and Richards, *The Privileged Planet*, 40 - 41.
9. Peter D. Ward and Donald Brownlee, *Rare Earth: Why Complex Life is Uncommon in the Universe* (New York: Copernicus, 2000), 220.
10. Gonzalez and Richards, *The Privileged Planet*, 50.
11. Ibid.
12. Ibid. 208.
13. Ibid.
14. Ibid. 334.
15. Richard Dawkins, "Science and God: A Warming Trend?," Science 277 (1997), 890.

Chapter 4
A World of Beauty and Awe

We appear to live, in the words of Gonzalez and Richards, on a privileged planet. If the argument of the foregoing chapter is valid, the planet we inhabit not only provides a rare combination of conditions enabling life of a highly complex nature to survive and thrive, but also ensures that the most highly developed form of life can satisfy its strange sense of curiosity about the larger universe in which it finds itself.

We have also noted that this developed sense of 'cosmic curiosity' is, speaking from a strictly evolutionary point of view, something of a biological luxury; an attribute of our mental life developed far beyond that which is necessary for biological survival. This alone makes it is an interesting oddity. However its strangeness is further compounded by nature's remarkable benignity in providing the means to satisfy this cosmic curiosity, namely, those anomalies that make Earth an unusually efficient observation platform. In short, nature has not only endowed us with a desire for discovery, but has also placed us in a naturally occurring laboratory beautifully designed for just such a purpose. Moreover, this 'laboratory' exists largely because of anomalous conditions existing on this planet. Despite what we have been taught about the Copernican Principle, the Earth is not representative of the universe at all.

But what is even more remarkable, the set of anomalies that allow life at our level of complexity to exist on Earth and the set that enables our cosmic curiosity to be sated are, by and large, the same! Because there is absolutely no reason to expect that this should be so, this fact is yet another deep mystery of existence, albeit one not often appreciated.

Yet, even Gonzalez and Richards do not go far enough. The anomalous nature of our planet does even more than mysteriously provide windows of observation. It also creates conditions which satisfy another biological luxury with which the human race has been endowed, namely, appreciation of beauty and awe. Not only is our planet privileged to be a platform of observation. It is also privileged to be an unusually clear window into the realm of the beautiful, the awesome and the sublime. Our planet is a very beautiful one. Furthermore—and for no apparent reason—the factors that enable this window into the appreciation of the beautiful to be wide open are, by and large, the same factors that we have already been considering as conducive to life and observation!

Let us look more closely at this assertion.

If we were to simply stop and look around at the things which thrill our souls and add beauty to our lives, what would we consider?

Flowers might be one of the things that come to the mind of many people. Birds might be another.

We might also think of a deep blue sky, maybe graced with fluffy white clouds or distant towers of thunderheads; or the ocean, deep blue with lines of white lacy waves breaking against the shore.

Or, having mentioned thunderheads, what can we say about a display of lightning and the awe-filled boom of crashing thunder?

Then again, will we overlook lofty mountain ranges, spectacularly capped with white layers of snow? Some would list these as the most sublime places on the planet.

Yet, although it might not be immediately obvious, everything that we have just mentioned in some manner has a bearing upon both the habitability of our planet and its suitability as a platform of discovery!

Considering the 'things bright and beautiful' just mentioned, essentially at random, we may immediately note the role that flowers—and plants in general—play in maintaining the atmospheric balance of this planet. Without plant life, there would be no oxygen for animals to breathe. But flowering planets have also played a very important role in the dating of ancient lake sediments through their content of Carbon-14. Charles Darwin once famously remarked that the excessive production of pollen occurring in the pant world demonstrates an extravagance in nature. The survival of plant species could have been ensured by a far less copious pollen production. Yet, it is this very extravagance which allows the use of pollen granules to date layered deposits. Had pollen production been less 'wasteful' the material available for scientists to study would have been too meager to ensure the accuracy of their age determinations.

Secondly, we mentioned birds as creatures having the power of inspiring us with a sense of beauty. Biologists have at times remarked that humans resemble birds more closely than mammals in certain respects, not just being bipedal, but more strikingly in our employment of sounds and musical notes. Most other mammals, by contrast, rely strongly on smells. Sounds are of less significance. There is little in common, for instance, between the way humans employ their voice in music (not even mentioning the enhancements through musical instruments) and the grunts of apes.

By contrast, the olfactory sense is employed relatively little by humans.

The mammals closest to humans in this respect are the Cetaceans; whales, porpoises and dolphins.

The colored plumage of many birds is also highly attractive to humans, as well as to other birds, and some species (for instance, the Bower Bird) even displays somewhat human-like attractions to 'pretty' things.

Birds are important in the ecological web of life, in part through their ability to spread plant seeds and in certain instances even assist in pollination. A mutually beneficial relationship exists between the plant world and certain members of the bird family.

One may not think that birds play a particularly important role in the intelligibility of the world, but it is almost certainly true that the desire for flight and the study of aerodynamics (and discoveries devolving from this) has benefited from our being surrounded by flying creatures. We may wonder if the desire for human flight would have eventuated at all, had there been no birds or other flying creatures. We might also note at this point how the notion of flight has long been associated with supernatural beings. Popular art typically depicts angels, for example, as sporting bird-like wings, even though there is very little support for this notion in the words of the Bible.

The beauty of a blue sky, of white clouds and towering thunderheads, depends upon the type of atmosphere enveloping our world. This vitally impinges upon the question of habitability. An atmosphere with few, if any, clouds would imply either a planet possessing very low water content or one so cold that most of its water had frozen out as surface ice (assuming water vapor clouds of course. Clouds of dust, dry ice or frozen methane such as observed on Titan could exist on waterless worlds).

As for establishing Earth as a suitable platform of discovery, an atmosphere that is transparent is necessary for humans to have knowledge of the wider universe. Thus, the kind of gaseous mantel capable of providing us with such a spectacular blue vault above our heads equally fulfils the exact requirement for astronomical discovery. We repeat our earlier remark that one could hardly imagine acquiring astronomical knowledge under a 'Venusian' sky!

Some of the most spectacular clouds are those in which the extremely high voltages triggering lightning flashes are generated. Lightning and its accompanying thunder, despite a relatively high rate of occurrence in most parts of the world, is not something that is easily dismissed through familiarity. It remains a truly awesome phenomenon revealing a side of nature both majestic and fearful. It is not for nothing that the hymn writer penned these words;

> I see the stars, I hear the roaring thunder
> Thy power throughout the universe displayed.

From time immemorial, thunder and lightning has, in poetical expression and prophetic vision, symbolized the awe and majesty of God. How frequently is God's wrath depicted by a lightning bolt? Even in our prosaic culture, there remains something about the power of a thunderstorm that calls to mind nature's awesome potential.

Of course, lightning is not confined to Earth-like situations. Jupiter supports bolts that dwarf anything we experience on Earth, and Saturn is likewise electrically active. But terrestrial lightning has a special importance for life on this planet by providing the energy needed to synthesize soluble nitrogenous compounds in our atmosphere and deliver them to the soils through rainfall. In effect, a thunderstorm supplies terrestrial vegetation with a light dose of the nitrogenous fertilizer necessary for the maintenance of a healthy ecosystem. Lightning continues to be the 'spark of life' on Earth. It may have actually assisted in the synthesis of organic compounds early in the life of our planet. As we saw earlier, opinions are changing about the composition of the very early terrestrial atmosphere, but if (in contradiction to most recent thinking on the subject) it turns out that the first atmospheric gases really were reducing, lightning and solar radiation may have contributed much of the planet's store of organic chemicals via the Miller-Urey process.

Although lightning has been known as long as there were human beings on this planet (maybe it was through observing a lightning strike that man discovered fire!) its study continues to reveal surprises. There is—rather surprisingly perhaps—still a lot to learn about the phenomenon. The exact mechanism by which electric charges are separated in a thunderstorm is still far from completely understood, and relatively recently, the existence of a high altitude counter discharge was discovered. Glows and even balls of light at the tops of thunderclouds have been reported anecdotally for decades, but the discoveries of the so-called 'sprites' came as an unexpected surprise.

More recently, there was an even bigger surprise with the discovery that lightning flashes emit bursts of X-rays. Cartoonists were apparently closer to the truth than anyone suspected by drawing lightning-strike victims with all their bones visible!

We are evidently nowhere near exhausting all the information about static electricity generation in the atmosphere, nor the phenomena associated with very energetic electrical discharges that this natural high-voltage laboratory can teach us.

From looking up at the sky, we turn our eyes downward to that other blue vault, the ocean. How drab our planet would be without the ocean!?

Indeed, but we would not be here to know anything about it!

As we saw earlier, not only is water in itself a necessary ingredient of a living planet, but an abundance of the substance is required to maintain a rich ecosystem and to adequately lubricate the process of plate tectonics; itself vital to the maintenance of complex life.

We also saw that a planet's stock of water cannot be too large if complex life is to be maintained. There must be enough to ensure deep oceans, yet not enough to drown the planet totally and create a water world.

Interestingly, we also saw how a deep (but less than global) ocean is optimum for the preservation of information in sedimentary layers. Gonzalez and Richards marveled at the way a water content that achieved the 'Goldilocks mean' between not-too-little and not-too-much was optimal both for habitability and measurability. We could add that a water content in this range is also best suited for the creation of vast oceans and spectacular shorelines; spectacular scenery of stunning beauty which can arouse feelings of awe not unlike that experienced in a thunderstorm; as well as, on other occasions, a sense of deep serenity. One who lives by the ocean will testify to the many moods of the sea and verify the truth of this statement. As we remarked above, our planet would be a far drabber place without it.

From the depths to the heights, we now cast our attention toward those festoons of majestic snow-crowned mountain ranges that wend their way across the landmasses of our world. These have always been held in awe by mankind. Ancient peoples held mountains to be the habitation of gods and supernatural beings; a belief still found amongst many people groups. This is probably inspired in part by the dramatic phenomenon of the glory. Glories are related to rainbows and occur when a light source behind the observer throws his shadow onto a bank of cloud, mist, or even onto the dewy coating of a lawn. Backscattering of light from tiny water droplets makes the area of mist ahead of an observer appear bright. If his shadow projects onto it, this will loom as a huge silhouette against the brighter background. The observer sees an enormous black figure surrounded by a brilliant and typically rainbow-colored halo of light, appear from the mist ahead of him. Many a mountain climber he been startled by such a huge haloed apparition and it is not surprising that such sightings by primitive peoples fuelled legends of mountain gods and giants.

But the awe of mountains is not by any means confined to the sporadic sightings of glories. The very nature of mountains themselves, so immense on a human scale of things, is enough to encourage a belief in super-human beings inhabiting their heights. Mountains are super-human in their majesty, so why should they not harbor super-human inhabitants? The glories only seemed to confirm this suspicion!

It is probably true to say that no other geographical feature can arouse a sense of awe in the way that mountains can. They make human beings and all our efforts seem very small. Moreover, major mountain chains are also accompanied by other phenomena which accentuate this sense of contrast between the mighty geographical features and we humans. Avalanches, sudden storms and high winds, earthquakes and, in certain mountainous areas, volcanoes all add to the almost forbidden aura of mountain regions.

On the other side of the coin, mountainous regions also display some of the most sublime of natural phenomena. Glaciers, majestic waterfalls and ever-changing cloudscapes fairly transport one into a fantasy land of light and sound.

We recall our earlier statement that mountain ranges of the fold variety are unique to the Earth in our solar system. Of course, mountain-like rims of impact craters and isolated volcanic formations (some larger than anything occurring on Earth) exist on other solar system planets, but the fold mountains that typify much terrestrial geology are a product of the plate tectonic activity whose continued existence differentiates our world from the other members of the Sun's family.

We have already spoken about the essential role that continuing plate tectonics plays in maintaining a suitable environment for complex terrestrial life, and we have also seen how it plays an important role in the acquisition of fundamental information about the Earth's interior. We may now, it seems, add to these the role that it plays in providing terrestrial inhabitants with some of their most beautiful and awe-inspiring sights!

Incidentally, a superterrestrial planet would be unable to support mountains as lofty as those of Earth, even if it happened to be as geologically active as our world. Once again there is correlation with habitability and discoverability, as these larger counterparts of Earth are unlikely to be favorable environments either for advanced life or as platforms of discovery. Only one such world is known at the time of writing, and it is especially uninviting; a fiercely hot planet huddled close to its parent star. There is however, no reason to think that others exist at distances from their stars comparable with that of Earth from the Sun.

We cannot speak about plate tectonics without our thoughts turning to earthquakes.

Nobody would call an earthquake beautiful, but they certainly inspire feelings of awe and fear. Of course, in the case of a severe quake, this sense of fear is very well founded, but several people have noted that there is also an irrational (or, perhaps it would be better to say "non-rational") fear which can be out of proportion to any clear threat to life or wellbeing.

Perhaps earthquakes deliver a blow to our subconscious sense of the security of the earth beneath our feet. If there is any security to be found in the physical world, surely (we feel) it is in the earth beneath us; the ground on which we stand secure. The atmosphere may rage with storm, the ocean may boil in the fury of a hurricane, but the solid land remains as a secure and solid foundation.

Then, without warning, this one secure foundation of the physical environment heaves and shakes!

Ripples run across it like wavelets on a pond and what appeared unmovable suddenly becomes fluid.

Perhaps there are other factors as well. Lyall Watson speculates that part of the fear induced by earthquakes might be triggered by the low-frequency vibrations preceding them. He notes that these vibrations occur within the frequency range that is known to induce feelings of anxiety in people and animals. Dogs have been noted as becoming agitated prior to an earthquake, in apparent support of this suggestion.

Watson himself recalls a personal experience of this non-rational fear. He writes that;

> I remember running outside during a small earthquake in Crete in 1967 and, despite the fact that I was perfectly safe out of doors and was fascinated by what was going on, feeling an irrational fear so deep-seated that I was unable to sleep indoors for more than a week.[1]

Watson was not, it seems, in any physical danger at the time, nor does his recollection of the incident suggest that he was even concerned about his safety per se. The fear that gripped him was, as he expresses it "irrational" and "deep-seated", almost like the awakening of some primordial phobia.

A different but equally interesting reaction was reported by philosopher and pioneer psychologist William James, an eyewitness to the severe San Francisco earthquake of April 18, 1906. James writes of his own reaction;

> The emotion consisted wholly of glee and admiration; glee at the vividness which such an abstract idea or verbal term as "earthquake" could put on when translated into sensible reality and verified concretely; and admiration at the way in which the frail little wooden house could hold itself together in spite of such a shaking. I felt no trace whatever of fear; it was pure delight and welcome.
> 'Go it,' I almost cried aloud, 'and go it stronger!'[2]

James goes on to speak of people sleeping out of doors for several nights following the quake, not only for safety from further tremors but also "to work off their emotions, and get the full unusualness out of the experience."

Here we appear to encounter a sort of transcendent experience that could without too much exaggeration be called a sense of 'beauty' in the experience; tragic, devastating and frightening though it certainly was.

A World of Beauty and Awe

Is there a pattern emerging?

Although some of the associations to which we have drawn attention may be criticized as being trivial—and taken alone probably are—the broader picture is beginning to look interesting. *The suitability of an environment for advanced life and its capability as a platform for discovery are not alone in being fundamentally interrelated. They also appear somehow correlated with the experience of the beautiful, the awe-full and the sublime.*

Perhaps the sample thus far is too small? Maybe the suspected correlation will disappear if a wider range of phenomena is examined?

Let us therefore, look at some other phenomena and see if the correlation still holds.

Total solar eclipses

Who can not be moved by the majestic sight of a total solar eclipse? It is surely a feast for the senses; the temperature drops as you watch a great wall of darkness move across your position on the Earth and you hear the gasps of the bystanders as they watch, awed by the amazing spectacle unfolding all around them. Even animals in the vicinity react in their own way. Scientist and peasant stand side by side, equally awed by this great cosmic drama. Astronomer Guillermo Gonzalez describes his experience:

> To experience a total solar eclipse is much more than simply to see it. The event summons all the senses. The dramatic drop in temperature was just as much a part of it as the blocked Sun. . . . Just after the total phase ended, many burst into spontaneous applause, as if rewarding a choreographer for a well-executed ballet.[3]

As discussed earlier, solar eclipses have not only contributed greatly to the advance of our knowledge of the universe; they also demonstrate in a very dramatic manner the strange co-incidence of apparent size between the Sun and Moon as observed from the surface of Earth. This, we argued, is more than an astronomical curiosity. There are very strong anthropic reasons why the apparent sizes of these two highly disparate bodies must be fine tuned to the degree that we see them to be. Not only would solar eclipses of the remarkably spectacular variety we witness on Earth be impossible without this remarkable 'co-incidence', but complex life itself appears to depend upon it!

Comets, meteors and meteorites.

Comets have always excited and terrified Earth's inhabitants. Not for nothing did Shakespeare include in his play *Julius Caesar*, the immortal lines;

> When beggars die, there are no comets seen
> The heavens themselves blaze forth the death of princes.

History records that there was a bright comet visible at the time of Caesar's death.

Even today that strange mixture of beauty and fear aroused by really spectacular comets has not died away. One prominent amateur astronomer remarked how the brilliant comet Hyakutake of 1996 would have aroused great fear in earlier ages, commenting that it appeared in the sky "like the finger of God".

As discussed earlier, the role of comets in Earth's habitability is presently under discussion. We know that they contain significant stores of both water and organic materials, but just how much of this contributed to the Earth's early store of these materials—and hence to life itself—is not as clear as the majority of scientists believed just a few years ago. If it is found that the Urey-Millar process was viable in the earliest terrestrial environment, the delivery of cometary organics may have been less important than supposed.

Nevertheless, it is unlikely that comets played no role in the accumulation of Earth's primitive store of organics. They contain a variety of very complex organic molecules, and it is difficult to imagine that the addition of these to the early Earth did not play an important role in preparing the way for life.

Moreover, there seems little doubt that comets and their 'first cousins', asteroids, played a significant role in the mass extinctions through which a succession of dominant species emerged. Ultimately, the mass extinction of the dinosaurs paved the way for the dominance of mammals and, eventually, humanity.

It is also true that there is a sense in which the existence of comets within a solar system may be seen as a gauge to the volatile and organic content of that system. That is to say, if a system of planets formed with little volatile material, comets would be rare. Life however, would be exceedingly unlikely in such a system.

Comets and asteroids have proven to be important repositories of material from earlier days of the Solar System. Asteroids can directly deposit fragments of themselves on Earth in the form of meteorites. The fall of a meteorite is, incidentally, another of nature's most dramatic spectacles of light and sound which earned for them the old name of 'thunderbolts'.

It is possible that some of the more friable meteorites originated in comets, but the bulk of cometary material is certainly too fragile to survive passage through the Earth's atmosphere. Nevertheless, dust grains resulting from disintegrated cometary material are collected in the atmosphere and we are already beginning to examine comets in situ, through the use of space probes. Much can also be learned about the composition of these bodies from spectroscopic study of the secondary products released into their nebulous heads and tails.

From these various studies, scientists conclude that cometary material is even more primitive than asteroidal and most would agree that by studying these objects, we are coming as close as we can to probing the composition of the very embryo of the Solar System.

Comets also played an important role in our understanding of the Solar Wind and magnetic fields in interplanetary space. Because their plasma tails are driven by the solar wind, they act as extremely sensitive 'solar windsocks' monitoring its velocity and turbulence.

Dust particles too large to be swept away by solar radiation into the dust tails of comets continue to follow the comet's orbit, spreading out behind it as a meteoroid stream. Although only a small percentage of comets have orbits that come close to that of Earth, nearly all that do and whose periods of revolution about the Sun are relatively short, are associated with meteor showers. As we pass close to their orbits, fragile crumb-sized particles get swept into our upper atmosphere and burn out high above Earth's surface as meteors or shooting stars. These particles are too small and fragile to reach the ground as meteorites and most of the meteor 'showers' are not really spectacular. Indeed if three shooting stars per hour appear to converge from a common spot in the sky, and can be shown to have been moving in similar orbits before striking the atmosphere, it is technically regarded as a meteor shower.

There are rare times, however, when Earth passes through an unusually dense cloud of meteoroids. When this happens, meteors appear in their thousands in what has come to be known as a meteor storm.

We should hasten to explain that "dense" is a relative term. The greatest meteor storms in recorded history dropped several hundred thousand meteors per hour, yet even here the average distance between individual particles was probably around twenty kilometers. One grain of sand every twenty kilometers is hardly a dense cloud by terrestrial standards, but it is very significant when compared with the low densities encountered in outer space.

The greatest storms ever recorded have been associated with the Leonid meteor stream, which in turn is associated with a rather lackluster comet known as Tempel-Tuttle. A drizzle of meteors is produced by this shower around the middle of November every year, but for a few years around the time of the comet's reappearance—every 32-33 years—the numbers increase dramatically and when the comet, meteor swarm and Earth are so related that the latter encounters the denser portions of the stream, spectacular storms of meteors are witnessed. In 1833 for instance, the meteors were described as falling like snowflakes in a snowstorm and in 1966, early risers in parts of the USA saw meteors falling at the rate of over twenty per second, rising to twice this number during a twenty minute period at the height of the storm. Following the comet's most recent appearance in 1998, meteor storms were seen in 1999, 2001 and 2002, although none became as intense as those of 1833 and 1966.

In earlier ages, these awesome events aroused great fear.

Thus, in 1366, the comet passed so close to Earth that it became a naked-eye object (rare for this particular comet) bright enough to attract the attention of official Chinese astronomers. For several days, the Chinese watched as the comet arced across the skies. Meanwhile, its debris strafed the upper atmosphere over Portugal. In the words of one chronicler;

> There was in the heavens a movement of the stars such as men never before saw or heard of . . . they fell from the sky in such numbers and so thickly together that . . . the air seemed to be in flames, and even the earth appeared as if ready to take fire.[4]

Behind the obvious fear expressed in these words, lies a genuine account of one of nature's most beautiful and awesome phenomena. Long before we invented pyrotechnic displays, nature had perfected the art.

Supernovas

The most violent of stellar phenomena, supernovas are truly awesome explosions that occur in galaxies about every 50 years or so. Whilst most stars die a quiet death, those destined to become supernova end their lives with catastrophic explosions of immense proportions, ejecting gas at speeds of up to 10,000 km/s and packing a luminous punch equivalent to 10 billion suns. What is outstanding for our discussion is that the very process that makes these events so awe inspiring is exactly what makes them conducive to Earth's habitability. In these enormous explosions iron, and elements heavier than iron, are fused. The very iron in our blood was synthesized in the furnace of a supernova!

The ejected gases from the explosion will eventually expand out into a gossamer nebula marking the grave of a once mighty star. The Crab Nebula in Taurus is a particularly beautiful remnant of a supernova; the one recorded by the Chinese in 1054 AD. That year the 'new' star blazed for several months, at its peak brightness outshining the planet Venus and visible even in broad daylight. After tens of thousands of years the chemically enriched gas will merge with other interstellar gas clouds. Eventually these will contract and give birth to a new generation of stars having a higher concentration of heavy elements. Thanks to supernovas, solar systems sufficiently enriched by heavy elements to allow both terrestrial and gaseous planets to form, are possible. In systems such as these, where rocky planets orbit relatively close to their sun and giant gaseous 'jupiters' act as shields against incoming comets, the minimum requirements for habitability are met.

Thus, not only are supernovas awe inspiring and their remnant nebulas beautiful; they actually help make possible the existence of the astronomers who observe and admire them!

We also add that supernova, because of their great intrinsic brilliance, enable these astronomers to judge the distances of remote galaxies, yielding some notion of the size of the universe and the vast distances between these mighty systems of stars. More recently, the careful monitoring of one particular type of supernova yielded the initial evidence (since then apparently confirmed by other astronomical studies) that the expansion of the universe is speeding up, not slowing as had previously been believed. This discovery is having serious repercussions in cosmology and, if finally confirmed, will be marked as a significant milepost in the growth of our knowledge of the universe.

Aurora

The magnificent 'Polar Lights' occur when charged particles from the Sun are funneled down into the Earth's upper atmosphere by our planet's magnetic field. As the particles collide with atoms and molecules in the atmosphere they excite bound electrons to higher energy levels ('orbits' within the atom). When an electron in an excited atom jumps back to its normal, unexcited, level it emits a photon. The combined effect of billions of these emitted photons gives us the northern and southern lights. These light displays of higher latitudes are more than beautiful sights in the sky. They provide evidence of the geomagnetic field's effectiveness in shielding Earth's surface from cosmic particles that would otherwise sterilize it.

But the geomagnetic field itself carries information about processes deep within the Earth. That is to say, as well as being necessary for the continuation of life on this planet, it is also a feature through which information about the planet itself is made available to the more curious and intelligent forms of life which it protects. Efforts to explain the existence of terrestrial magnetism have stimulated major research into the planet's interior.

Rainbows.
Rainbows are far more than just pretty sights in the sky. They depend on our finely tuned atmosphere, but, as Gonzalez and Richards remark,[5] they have also indirectly aided in our understanding of the universe by providing an example, in nature, of the spectrum. Through this, the true nature of white light is revealed. Knowledge of the spectrum has, furthermore, provided one of the most fruitful windows into the understanding of the universe, including the composition of stars (once thought to be a forever insoluble problem) and through the Doppler Effect, knowledge of the motions of stars and galaxies and even the universal expansion leading to the formulation of the Big Bang creation theory. Not for nothing has the spectroscope been called the greatest invention ever made, yet a basic model was already present in the natural world in the form of the rainbow!

A miscellany of beauty and awe!
Let us not forget the awe-inspiring pristine night sky. A night sky like ours is only possible because we are in a neighborhood of relatively low stellar population. But that too is necessary for the habitability of our planet. A region with significantly more stars would hold greater dangers such as nearby supernovas and comet showers resulting from close approaches by neighboring stars or clouds of interstellar matter. Probably all solar systems similar to our own are surrounded by vast haloes of comets susceptible to disruption by close encounters with other stars or interstellar clouds.

On the other hand, a sky largely devoid of stars would imply a location in the outer reaches of the Galaxy where, as we have already seen, planet-building heavy elements exist in far weaker concentrations than in the solar neighborhood.

Even supposing that we could survive in such an environment, a sky crowded with brilliant stars and nearby gaseous nebula would largely prevent our wider, extragalactic, view of the universe while a region in the sparser outer limits of the Galaxy would have the unfortunate consequence of many interesting astronomical denizens of this great star system being too far away for easy observation.

Mention of the extragalactic perspective reminds us that the views of other galaxies themselves are something that cannot help but induce a feeling of the immensity of the universe.

Although spectacular photographs of galaxies adorn the average book on astronomy, we cannot say that the view of one of these objects through the eyepiece of a telescope is an especially awe-inspiring experience in itself. The ones highlighted in the typical coffee table astronomy book are the more photogenic of their class and even these look more spectacular in photographs than through the eyepiece. Typically, what is seen at the eyepiece end of a telescope is a faint fuzzy blob with little apparent detail.

The true significance lies in the realization of what this blob of light actually is.

It is nothing less than the unresolved glow of tens or even hundreds of billions of stars; fierce thermonuclear furnaces like our Sun, spread across tens of thousands of light years of space in a vast self-gravitating system, tens of millions of light years from Earth. Moreover, the light entering our eyes tonight left those multitudinous stars millions of years before human beings walked this Earth. What appears as an inconspicuous blob of misty light is actually a revelation of both the vastness of space and the immensity of time.

Here, awe and knowledge meet. The awe inspired by this seemingly insignificant blob of glowing mist is not a consequence of its appearance (as might be the case for a brilliant aurora or bright comet), but comes through knowledge of the object's true nature. Without the discoveries of the past eighty years or so, our position would be no different from that of Charles Messier who initially mistook galaxies for faint comets within the Solar System. When his suspected comets failed to show movement, he casually catalogued them to prevent himself and other comet hunters mistakenly reporting them as new discoveries!

In a similar vein, albeit on a more fundamental level, advances in physics increasingly disclose a basic symmetry in the laws of nature, revealing in these a beauty manifesting through the mathematical formulations describing them. The phrase "beautiful mathematics" may not be appreciated by everyone, but it is a phrase which constantly turns up in the writings of physicists. In fact, this concept of 'beauty' is used as one criterion by which a theory is judged. If a theory lacks beauty—if it is manifestly ad hoc, lacks symmetry and does not fit harmoniously into the set of theories describing the natural world—it will be judged by most physicists as being almost certainly incorrect, even if it appears to account for the phenomenon in question. It may be retained as a temporary solution for practical purposes, but only until a better theory comes along, probably following a new discovery which will shed further light on a deeper and more fundamental level of the physical universe. Such was the case with Newton's Theory of Gravity. It worked well, but remained 'inelegant' or ad hoc in so far as it effectively pulled a force out of thin air as it were, without really explaining why such a force should exist at all. On a more metaphysical level, it left unanswered the thorny question as to what the word "force" really denotes in the first place. *Ad hoc* entities such as gravitational forces were subsequently made redundant by Einstein's more comprehensive, elegant and beautiful General Theory of Relativity.

The progress of physics continues to be one of discovering increasingly comprehensive and beautiful laws. Although the non-physicist may be hard pressed to appreciate this fact (just as someone with distorted optical perception may not appreciate the beauty of a Constable or a Blake), the physicist sees each new step along the road of discovery as revealing an increasingly beautiful universe.

In the words of one of their number, University of Delaware Professor Stephen Barr,

> The story of science is in many ways like the old fairy tale in which the hero is confined by a witch to the bottom of a dark well, but discovers there by luck and courage the secret entrance to her subterranean storehouse. Deep under the fields and forests he finds unimaginable treasures of rare beauty. Little did the old researchers in science, labouring over foul-smelling test tubes or experimenting with magnets and coils of wire, imagine what secret beauty lay at the bottom of the deep well of nature.[6]

The Secret Beauty of Creation

This of course raises the question "From whence does this 'secret beauty' originate?"

The process of science always explains the limited as a consequence of the deeper and more general. Therefore, it appears inevitable that at the end of this road there must be a fundamental theory in which all the beauty of physical law is gathered. By "theory" in this context we mean something objective; a law of nature, not just a hypothesis in the human mind. In a sense, theories are discovered rather than constructed or, to be more accurate, the theories conceived by human minds are ever-greater approximations to the ultimate Theory of Everything; the way in which the physical world exists. In this sense, the Theory exists irrespective of whether anyone ever formulates it. It is simply the way things ultimately *are*. The discovery of this Ultimate Theory will actually be the discovery of the complete and accurate mathematical description of the physical world. As yet, the mathematical descriptions are only partially correct. As we say, the theories yet formulated are incomplete and to a greater or lesser degree inaccurate. The wonder is, the more accurate the theories become, the correspondingly greater the fundamental mathematical beauty of the universe is seen to be. Quoting Barr once more "if at the end of the road one is confronted with a magnificent example of what we called 'symmetric structure' in the ultimate laws themselves, then science really has no alternative to offer to the Argument from Design."[7] All evidence suggests that science is traveling down a path leading to this very conclusion.

So what have we here?

Like the Earth, the universe itself appears fine tuned for life, discovery and beauty. The basic laws of nature allow for the existence for an island of life such as Earth. But these very same laws are seen to manifest a deep and fundamental beauty that can only be revealed through scientific discovery of the most fundamental kind. We find ourselves in profound agreement with the great mathematical physicist Hermann Weyl that "in our knowledge of physical nature we have penetrated so far that we can obtain a vision of the flawless harmony which is in conformity with sublime reason."[8]

Cosmic beauty; cosmic awe

Earlier, we referred to 'cosmic curiosity' as being, in a sense, an 'abstract' curiosity. It is not a curiosity that deals with specific situations, such as the biologically useful curiosity about which berries are edible and which are poisonous. It is now becoming apparent that if this cosmic curiosity is allowed to lead us into ever deeper investigation of "the nature of Nature", we will arrive at an equally abstract and equally cosmic beauty; a beauty not simply of the physical universe as it manifests to the senses, but beauty of an even more fundamental and—if the word is not too inappropriate in this context—'esoteric' kind . . . a beauty of the very laws by which this universe functions and which are ultimately only expressible in the form of mathematical equations. For those with eyes to see it, these equations bespeak the most profound and subtle of beauties.

We might also note, once again, that the more cosmic and abstract all this becomes, the further it shifts from anything of biological survival value or even practical application. The beauty of personal adornment no doubt possessed survival value in early societies, as it was used then (as today) to attract members of the opposite sex. But there would be negative survival value for an early hunter and gatherer to become so absorbed in the contemplation of a beautiful mountain range that he failed to notice a lion stalking him! And the beauty of the mathematics of nature's most fundamental laws totally escaped early human society.

Yet, just as modern society spends huge sums of money on pure scientific research, it also spends relatively large sums on the beautification of city parks, art galleries and even on the construction of roads through barely accessible and frequently dangerous mountain country for no other purpose than to construct a lookout from where travelers can enjoy spectacular views of the surrounding countryside.

Indeed, it is probably not an exaggeration to say that pure scientific research itself is ultimately driven by the quest for that most abstract and cosmic of all beauties. Curiosity itself may be a quest for the ultimate beauty!

Beauty, not so much the delicate beauty of a rose petal, but the grand beauty of a mighty canyon or mountain range, passes imperceptibly into that difficult-to-define property of 'awesomeness' which affects the human spirit with a sense of our physical smallness and helplessness in the face of something far more powerful and majestic than ourselves. This is a kind of beauty, but not what we might call a 'soft' or 'gentle' or 'comforting' one. It is, nevertheless, far closer to the beauty that the mathematical physicist finds revealed in his equations of the basic functions of the universe. The observational astronomer may sense something of the awesome size of the universe, but the mathematical physicist uncovers the equally awesome and arguably even more beautiful symmetry underlying it all.

There exists a woodcut dating from the late 1800s that has appeared in many books on the history of astronomy over the years. Many authors who included it in their books assumed it to date from the Middle Ages and to represent an accurate depiction of the prevailing beliefs of those times. However we now know that it is more in the nature of a Nineteenth Century satire of the allegedly pre-Copernican point of view.

The woodcut depicts a flat earth, around which the dome of the sky rotates. On the edge of the scene, an intrepid traveler reaches the horizon where the stars set and, poking his head through the celestial sphere, observes the hidden mechanism which runs the universe!

Now, we earlier saw how such a 'small cosmos' picture actually caricatures the real pre-Copernican world view, but in an ironic sort of way, the woodcut applies more to the world view of the early Twenty First Century than to the Middle Ages. The Traveler is replaced by the mathematical physicist who, in a metaphorical sense, also pokes his head through the celestial sphere to view the mechanism behind it all. Except that the mechanism that is now glimpsed is something so abstract and beautiful as to require a mind of both exquisite mathematical skill and fine aesthetic sensitivity to truly appreciate what is but dimly perceived.

The view beyond the celestial sphere is still far from clear. But as research advances it comes little by little into greater focus and with increasing clarity is revealed in ever greater beauty and awe. A wonder equal to that of the universe itself is that it lies within the appreciation and comprehension of the human mind. Fred Hoyle once expressed skepticism that the human brain's limit for processing information would be sufficient to comprehend of the universe's complexity and J. B. S. Haldane's aphorism that the universe is not only stranger than we suppose, but stranger than we can suppose is well known and frequently quoted. Yet, the human mind appears remarkably capable of interpreting the universe.

It is within this sense of awe, especially in its more 'cosmic' dimension, that we locate a 'religious' dimension to human experience. All beauty has a sort of 'transporting' effect upon us. When we experience something beautiful, we are for a moment lifted, as it were, above the common place; a purer and altogether lovelier side of existence is revealed to us. In the experience of awe, this sense of transport is intensified, sometimes to a frightening degree. It is this transporting experience of beauty, and especially of awe, that can be called 'religious' in the broadest sense of the term. In lifting us above ourselves, it carries us a little closer to another and more transcendent realm which always seems to lurk at the very periphery of consciousness; hard though we might try to make it go away!

We may ask why, of all the beings on this planet, humans alone experience a 'religious' dimension of life.

Is it simply that we alone have a sufficient degree of consciousness of self to feel the threat posed by our limitations in space and (especially) in time? In other words, is it a response to our feelings of vulnerability in the face of forces larger than us and the inevitability of our own death? Do we turn to imaginary gods and other supernatural beings in the hope that they might somehow help us if we successfully appease them?

A naturalistic outlook blended with some sophomore psychology might conceivably make such an argument, but it too lightly brushes aside vast areas of human experience.

What ever else may have nurtured the religious sense, surely the 'numinous' —the sense of awe—played a large role. What ever one may feel about the validity or otherwise of religious doctrines, one cannot dismiss the fact that people do report numinous experiences; 'religious' experiences which have less to do with personal finitude or mortality than with the awe and beauty of the world pressing in on the human psyche until it may almost overwhelm it.

Once again we encounter this strange apparent coincidence of certain properties of the world, unexpectedly endowing our lives with a greater richness. There is no obvious reason why this should be so. It is simply another of those bald facts of nature that mysteriously work in our favour.

The production of robots composed of meat—functioning biological organisms but without any profound degree of consciousness or any appreciation of such luxuries as beauty, awe or the numinous—would seem an entirely sufficient product of natural selection. Why do we even desire to 'peer behind the celestial sphere at the mechanism that is moving it', let alone appreciate the beauty that we find there?

Someone will undoubtedly pounce upon our assertion that the beauty we find in nature, whether in the flower of a rose or in the fundamental equations of physics, is something objective; something belonging to the natural world itself. "Is beauty not merely part of our subjective experience?" they will ask.

Unfortunately, we have so often been told that "Beauty is in the eye of the beholder" that many have come to accept the subjective nature of beauty as an intuitively obvious fact. However, a moment's thought should be enough to expose the flaw in this line of thinking.

Consider something of great beauty; an orchid flower for instance. Where is the property of beauty located, in the flower or in the subjective experience of the beholder? Is an orchid blooming in the depths of a primeval rainforest any less beautiful for never having been seen by mortal eyes?

If it is not in the flower itself, somehow the subjective experience of the person seeing the flower is beautiful, while the flower itself—the object of the experience of beauty—is not. This is simply nonsense.

It is no use appealing to disagreements about what things are and are not beautiful, as evidence favoring a subjective doctrine of beauty. There are also disagreements about what is good, but that does not mean that there is no objective goodness. We may even imagine somebody with a particular optical distortion disagreeing with us about which patterns are square. Yet, few people would use this as evidence for a subjectivist theory of geometry.

Moreover, when two people disagree over whether something is or is not beautiful, it is mainly in the sense that each thinks the other's idea of beauty is in some way distorted. A painting that one person thinks a masterpiece is rejected as "rubbish" by another. However, the very nature of the disagreement actually precludes aesthetic relativism. The person disagreeing about the beauty of a painting does not say something like "If you say it is beautiful, then it is to you, but I cannot see the beauty in it that you see". In most instances, the reaction is more like "I can't understand why you think that mess is beautiful!"

It is also significant that those disagreeing over whether something is or is not beautiful do not necessarily locate beauty in the experience alone. One may admit that beauty may be present in something, yet not apparent to one's own eyes. This is how most non-mathematical people feel about the physicist's talk of "beautiful mathematics".

It is also important to note however, that there is actually quite a remarkable *agreement* about what is beautiful; an agreement crossing even the lines of times and cultures. In all of the arts, extending across long periods of time, there has been strong agreement that symmetry is beautiful, even that it may contain the very essence of beauty. Geometrical symmetries are found in all manner of decorative patterns such as friezes, tilings, architecture and the like, from a wide variety of epochs and cultures. In music, arithmetical symmetry is basic to the scales of notes, as well as in meter and rhythm. It also occurs in the metrical and rhyme schemes of poetry and in the patterns of dance. As in art, so in nature, symmetry is seen as beauty across times and cultures. If beauty really did exist only in the eye of the beholder, it is strange that so many eyes of such a multitude of different beholders should be so mutually attuned.

Furthermore, it is not readily apparent how a subjectivist view of beauty, even if viable, could alleviate the difficulty of why humans possess such a developed sense of the beautiful. It would remain obscure as to why certain objects in the natural world, and certain properties of that world itself, should induce even the subjective experience of beauty in our minds. The sense of beauty remains as much a biological luxury as ever.

Our Place in the World

In the light of what has been said above, how do we assess the world and our place within it?

Do we, as the 'Copernicans' insist, find a natural order that appears totally indifferent to the existence of human beings? Does it seem merely an accident that we inhabit this planet and not some other; whether in this Solar System or elsewhere?

Or do we find that the natural order seems somehow to favour us and nurture us? Do we find that this Earth gives the appearance of having been (in some sense) 'prepared' for our habitation? Do we find that we have been mysteriously endowed with the biological luxuries of cosmic curiosity and an appreciation of a strange but pervasive property called beauty that gives the universe an extra dimension of significance and which, in some equally mysterious way, even seems to underlie the fundamental laws of nature themselves?

Unless we have totally succumbed to an educational system which simply denies the latter as an act of faith, we must surely see nature in the light of the second alternative.

But here we encounter a problem whose existence the first alternative does not even admit. It is the same mystery which has come to light several times already . . . why should the universe 'care' for us and nurture us in this way? Why should the universe be such that the emotion of cosmic curiosity arises in such small and apparently insignificant creatures as us *and* why should the universe be such that this emotion is capable of satisfaction? Why should we have an appreciation of beauty, when we could have functioned quite well without it (as, indeed, we could have functioned equally well without cosmic curiosity) *and* why should the universe be such as to display beauty even down to the level (we might even say *especially* down to the level!) of the most basic laws of physics?

To be honest, it looks as though this whole situation is, as Fred Hoyle allegedly remarked in a slightly different but closely related context, "a put up job"! It looks as though the sense of beauty and this emotion of cosmic curiosity (which, as suggested, also appears to depend upon a sense of beauty at a basic level) has in some manner been programmed within our very genes, for the purpose of discovering the basic beauty and harmony of the universe itself.

Is the universe itself possessed of an intelligence that deliberately fashioned us in such a way that we would admire its own beauty?

There is nothing about the material universe suggesting the intrinsic possession of a mind. However if we assume for the sake of argument that the ancient Stoics and there modern counterparts were right and that intelligence is intrinsic to the material world, it would appear to have ultimately failed if its purpose was to direct us to the contemplation of the beauty of the universe and not look any further. It over shot the mark so to speak, in so far as the contemplation of the greatest and most majestic beauty translates into a sense of numinous that by its nature points to something beyond the physical universe. It implies some ultimate resting place for that deepest of human desires; a desire that transcends the entire natural order as surely as it transcends the finite individual.

The Intelligence who "put up" the "job" is not a universal mind in the Stoic sense. Intelligence capable of decreeing that the fundamental laws of the universe are beautiful must of necessity transcend the natural realm. Remarkably, within the creation described by these laws is found at least one oasis capable of nurturing living organisms desirous of seeking the meaning and beauty of the created order; a beauty and order which, in the final analysis, points these seekers beyond the created order and back to the Source of it all.

Furthermore, this Source is clearly more than a deist First Cause who may well have created us with a sense of beauty and a cosmic curiosity, only to have us forever frustrated in a universe indifferent to such matters. On the contrary, the mysterious 'coincidence' that our desire for beauty, and cosmic curiosity, may be satisfied by the general nature of the universe and the highly anomalous situation of Earth finds satisfactory explanation only if there is, not merely an Intelligent Designer but a *Loving* Designer?

Seeing this situation as a "put up job" is actually recognizing it as an example of TC on a truly cosmic scale. It suggests that we have been nurtured in a specially prepared oasis, and programmed with certain desires, as well as having been given a high degree of consciousness. The latter is also a biological luxury, as we could surely survive without it. Nevertheless, a level of consciousness of this order *is* necessary if the biological luxuries of a sense of beauty, cosmic curiosity and the spiritual sense of numinous awe are to function. It seems that all of this has been arranged so that we could respond to the surrounding universe in particular ways. But for this response to occur, certain prerequisites must be met by the universe and our location within it. The oasis of life also needed to be a good platform of observation and a suitable gallery of the beautiful. There is no *a priori* reason why these different sets of criteria should coincide, any more than there is any *a priori* reason why an arrow painted on a parking lot floor should point to the exist. The latter points toward the exit because it was intelligently designed to do so. It has a TC which is the hallmark of intelligent design. But the former reveals a similar TC and therefore, ipso facto, must also be the product of intelligent design.

We may think of this in terms of our earlier remarks about the Earth's position on the multi-dimensional graph. It was argued that the region of habitability on this hypothetical graph appears to be very small. We pictured it in terms of a tiny target drawn on the surface of a vast wall. Into this tiny target, the arrows of discoverability, beauty and a form of life with a sense for both have been fired. Does this remind us of the 'target on the wall' model of Dembski's specified complexity? It does indeed seem like this to me, and I would furthermore point out that the dimensions of the 'target' have been set by the parameters of habitability and not drawn in after the arrows have been fired!

The design is intelligent; the purpose of that design loving. We therefore suggest that together they point toward a Designer whose nature is at least compatible with the God of the Bible. The identity of the 'Loving Designer' cannot be proven in the strict sense, but here we probably go as far as scientific reasoning and philosophical speculation can take us toward the Biblical God.

Possible Misunderstandings of this Position

The above conclusions will undoubtedly be controversial. Many will remain unconvinced.

Another possible misconception is of considerable importance and requires discussion at some length.

In brief, I do not subscribe to the position called 'Young Earth Creationism' and the argument presented here is not to be seen as in any way supporting that position. I accept the discoveries of science that set the age of the universe as close to fourteen billion years and that of the Earth at around 4.5 billion.

Although it would be an overstatement to say that the Big Bang origin of the universe has been proven beyond all doubt (very well-established scientific theories have in the past been totally overthrown by new evidence), the weight of evidence available at the present time very strongly supports the theory. As more data is accumulated, the theory is strengthened further. On these grounds, we can say that the Big Bang theory very probably describes the real history of the universe. In other words, barring some radical new discovery, we can be pretty sure that the universe began in an extremely hot and highly compressed state almost fourteen billion years ago; that it has been expanding and cooling ever since, and that all the galaxies, stars, planets and living entities existing today are composed of material which condensed from the sea of radiation following this event.

Modifications to the simple Big Bang theory, most notably Inflationary Theory postulating a very brief burst of exponential expansion of the infant universe, have been put forward in an attempt to clear up various problems that have arisen, not with the basic concept so much as the finer details. Several varieties of Inflation exist and as yet there is no consensus as to which, if any, is correct.

The Big Bang cosmology is not, however, a theory of origins per se. It is really a theory of what happened after the Big Bang creation event; how the universe passed from the dense sea of radiation immediately following its creation to the complex system of today. It is, essentially, an *evolutionary* theory, though not of course in the Darwinian sense.

As to what caused the Big Bang, or even what the Big Bang really was, ideas are much more speculative. This is not surprising, as the questions raised here are as much philosophical and even theological as they are scientific.

Of course the metaphysical naturalist, who in this day and age is also a materialist, finds the Big Bang an embarrassment unless he can explain it in terms of the laws of physics. But think about this for a moment. What *are* the laws of physics? If there were no universe, would there still be laws of physics?

It is difficult, if not downright impossible, for the materialistic naturalist to maintain that the laws of physics can, in some sense, exist apart from the physical reality which they describe. The only way would be to place them in some kind of Platonic Ideal realm where they exist as abstractions (what philosophers call universals) apart from the world of particulars. This theory is still naturalistic, but it is hardly compatible with a metaphysical materialism of the type demanded by today's full-blown scientific naturalist (it also has its own problems, but discussion of these would take us beyond the scope of this book). To be consistent, the naturalist appears forced to admit that the laws of physics are idealized descriptions of the way that the physical world functions. They cannot exist unless they are—in a manner of speaking—embodied in physical reality itself. Physical laws do not exist apart from the world as a *prescriptive* set of rules which any physical reality must follow. Rather, they are *descriptive* of how physical reality actually does behave.

But if this is true, how can they explain the *genesis* of this same physical reality?

If physical laws are descriptive of the material universe, they necessarily came into being with that universe. A description cannot exist prior to or apart from the thing described. Therefore, physical laws are incapable of describing the creation event; the passage from Absolute Nothingness to Something!

This issue is fudged somewhat by an ambiguity in the word "nothing". We use it here in the plain sense of total absence of any existing thing . . . where "thing" itself is defined in the widest possible sense. However, the word is also used by physicists in a less radical sense, namely, to describe the state of the quantum vacuum. This latter sense of the word has given rise to some interesting speculation.

One of the first things that anyone learns in the study of quantum theory is that the vacuum is *not* 'nothing'!

According to quantum theory, if we were to take a region of so-called empty space and evacuate every stray atom and every sub-atomic particle, if we were to shield it totally from every photon of light and screen out all electromagnetic waves and fields; if we even managed somehow to shield it from the gravitational pull of distant masses, and chilled it to absolute zero, the energy within that region of space would still not be zero!

One of the basic tenets of quantum theory, the Heisenberg Uncertainty Principle, states that the exact energy contained within this region of space cannot be specified with certainty, *ergo*, it cannot be specified as exactly zero. It actually fluctuates over a range of values and, esoteric though this prediction may sound, the effects of such fluctuations have actually been detected experimentally. These are the vacuum fluctuations that, quantum theory predicts, pervade the entire universe.

Now, these fluctuations are known to create sub-atomic particles—electrons and positrons which immediately annihilate each other—but the Uncertainty Principle implies that there is a very small but finite probability that something more massive could also emerge spontaneously from the quantum vacuum. Some cosmologists have seized upon this as a possible explanation for the Big Bang. In other words, the Big Bang was triggered by the mother of all quantum fluctuations!

Now, the reader will immediately see that this does not really explain the origin of the universe per se. At best, it might explain the origin of the material contents of the present universe. But the Big Bang was initially proposed as an explanation for the origin, not just of matter, but of space and time as well. The observed phenomenon of the expansion of space at cosmic dimensions demands as much. Although difficult to picture, the well-known recession of external galaxies is not due to these objects rushing away from each other within a fixed spatial framework. It is actually a manifestation of the expansion of the spatial framework itself. Extrapolating back into time, we arrive at a time when *space itself* is contracted to a point. This is quite different from the material universe being contracted to a point in a space that may still be of infinite extent. Yet if the quantum vacuum was supposed to exist prior to the Big Bang, the latter was strictly speaking not the origin of the universe. A reason for the 'empty', fluctuating quantum vacuum universe still has to be found.

This problem is, however, blurred by referring to the quantum vacuum as "nothing". The meaning of "nothing" easily jumps from its familiar radical meaning to its more restrictive quantum one, and back again, in this discussion.

Particle physicist Stephen Barr compares these two senses of "nothing" with the differences between a bank account having a zero balance and no bank account at all. In one sense, there is no difference. An empty account or no account both imply no money. But the very fact of having a bank account (even an empty one) presupposes a great deal that a complete lack of bank account does not. It presupposes a banking system, for example, which in turn implies the existence of a certain type of social order, political structure and so forth. This socio-political system requires an explanation, as does the origin of the bank account itself. Clearly, the bank account is not 'nothing', even though there may be no actual money deposited within it.[9]

Suppose, now, that the owner of the account has a windfall and deposits ten thousand dollars in his account. This becomes a relatively easy transaction, without the need for anything new being created. He is not opening an account, only depositing money in one. The situation would be different however, if he acquired this money and did not possess a bank account. In that instance, something new would need to be created.

With respect to the Big Bang, it seems that evidence points to a new 'bank account' having being created. By contrast, the hypothesis asserting that the Big Bang resulted from a quantum fluctuation only asserts that newly acquired wealth has been deposited in a pre-existing—albeit previously empty—account.

Indeed, *any* theory attempting to explain the Big Bang in terms of natural law is merely making this assertion. All such theories leave the existence of the 'bank account' unexplained.

Before leaving this topic of quantum fluctuations, we should mention that, although most physicists assume that the Heisenberg Principle and the vacuum fluctuations which it predicts are simply bald facts of nature, at least one physicist—Harold Puthoff—has put forward an explanation which sees both as the result of a feed-back process continuing all the time throughout the universe.[10]

Puthoff draws attention to the slight 'jitter' motion of sub-atomic particles within a sea of electromagnetic quantum fluctuations, to which Erwin Schroedinger gave the name "zitterbewegung". Puthoff argues that zitterbewegung is not merely the result of quantum fluctuations; it is also responsible for their generation. These fluctuations are, he suggests, an inevitable product of the 'jitter' of charged particles, but they also cause neighboring particles to 'jitter' and so maintain the process. On this view, it is this constant disturbance at the smallest scales of reality that generates vacuum fluctuations and maintains the basic uncertainty of quantum nature that W. Heisenberg enshrined in his Principle. Presumably, this process was set off in the Big Bang itself.

This brings us to an interesting point. If even the fluctuations in the quantum vacuum and Heisenberg's Principle themselves are products of the Big Bang, they can hardly be used to explain why the 'Bang' occurred in the first place!

Strangely, it appears that Puthoff missed seeing this consequence of his own suggestion. In the very same article he suggested that the Big Bang may have arisen from vacuum fluctuations. In the light of his own speculations, this position would seem to be very difficult to uphold . . . equally difficult, we might say, as the position of any scientist who tries to explain the Big Bang itself in terms of the physical laws which it generated!

A further possible misunderstanding of our position, viz. that our argument for the special preparation of Earth implies that other planets have not similarly been prepared, needs only a brief reply. The point is not that we are alone in the universe, but that *even we* would not be here if nature had simply been allowed to take its course devoid of the various apparent coincidences rendering our planet anomalous in many ways. What this does imply is that we cannot argue from the fact of our own existence to the *inevitability* of other similar beings elsewhere. The *possibility* of such beings remains, nevertheless, an open question.

It may also be objected that when we spoke of appreciation of beauty and cosmic curiosity as having been programmed into our genes, we appeared to suggest a 'miraculous' infusion of these characteristics into the human psyche. We do not, however, attempt to give any opinion as to the processes by which these psychological characteristics came about. It is only argued that whatever processes were involved, a Designing Intelligence was, in a manner of speaking, 'overseeing' the proceedings. Although I do not accept the thesis that natural selection and Darwinian evolutionary processes explain all the phenomena of biology, I am far from arguing that these processes play no role at all or that evolution per se does not occur. It not infrequently happens in science that some mechanism is found that beautifully explains a range of hitherto inexplicable phenomena. It is then assumed that, because the mechanism in question has been so successful in explaining these phenomena, it must be equally capable of solving a still wider range of mysteries; just about everything that is even vaguely related to the original subjects explained. Almost inevitably, this proves to be too ambitious. For example, it is interesting and vaguely amusing to browse through late Nineteenth Century copies of *Nature* or similar science journals and see how often the vague phrase "electrical phenomenon" is used as an explanation for everything from unusual luminous sky phenomenon to unexplained noises. I am not alone in suspecting that natural selection is being similarly used by biologists today as the explanation for just about every biological phenomenon encountered. Certainly, it is a valid explanation of many things (the emergence of antibiotic-resistant 'superbugs' in hospitals and the general phenomenon of microevolution—literally, the 'origin of the species'— is well explained by natural selection), but has it become to contemporary biology what "electrical phenomena" became to the scientists of the late Nineteenth Century?

This, however, brings us to wider issues whose pursuit would take us beyond the scope of this book.

It may also be objected that we appear to be holding humanity as the reason for the creation of the universe. This is simply not true. Although we do affirm that human beings are not accidental by-products of the universe, this does not imply that the universe was created solely for the purpose of providing a home for humanity. There is nothing illogical in believing that the Creator of this universe planned every part of it and that this planning included the existence of intelligent beings. This is not an arrogant assertion. *Every* part of the universe may have been planned with equal precision. We repeat the words of physicist Paul Davies "If physics is the product of design, the universe must have a purpose, and the evidence of modern physics suggests strongly to me that the purpose includes us."[11] Notice, however, that Davies said "includes us", not "is wholly concerned with us"!

The existence of humanity may be one of the reasons for the creation of the universe, but there are probably billions of other reasons as well, most of which will be forever unknown to us and no doubt would be incomprehensible even if we could know them. Maybe the Creator's overriding reason is to provide a partial revelation of his power and glory. Humanity, and whatever other intelligent creatures there may be, form part of this revelation, as well as being the 'observers' of it. We are the ones to whom the Creator's glory in and through creation has been displayed and to whom have been given the abilities to see something of it and to respond in worship. If we are to worship the Creator and Designer— God—with body, mind and spirit as the Bible commands us, part of this 'mental' worship surely involves the fulfilling of our sense of cosmic curiosity and thirst for beauty. In other words, the characteristically human pursuits of art, aesthetics and pure scientific research are not divorced from the equally uniquely human drive of worship. These pursuits are truly part of our worship of God, even though for many people they have become alienated from their spiritual source. Perhaps the time has come to recognize the essentially spiritual nature of science, the arts and aesthetics in general; to recognize the aesthetic quest as the deep motivation behind scientific research and, at an even deeper level, the subconscious and deeply suppressed longing for God as the ultimate motivation of aesthetics.

Notes

1. Lyall Watson, *Supernature: The Natural History of the Supernatural* (London: Hodder and Stoughton, 1973), 95.
2. Quoted in Frank W. Lane, *The Elements Rage: The Extremes of Natural Violence* (Newton Abbot: David & Charles, 1966), 179.
3. Guillermo Gonzalez and Jay Richards, *The Privileged Planet: How Our Place in the Cosmos is Designed for Discovery* (Washington DC: Regnery Publishing, 2004), 3.
4. Mark Littmann, *The Heavens on Fire: The Great Leonid Meteor Storms* (Cambridge: Cambridge University Press, 1998), 61.
5. Gonzalez and Richards, *The Privileged Planet* 69.
6. Stephen Barr, Modern Physics and Ancient Faith (Notre Dame, In: University of Notre Dame Press, 2003), 106.
7. Ibid.
8. Ibid. 109.
9. Ibid. 277-278.
10. Harold Puthoff, "Everything for Nothing" New Scientist 1727 (28 July, 1990), 52.
11. Paul Davies, *Superforce: The Search for a Grand Unified Theory of Nature* (London: Unwin Paperbacks, 1985), 243.

Appendix I
The Sensus Divinatis

Sensus divinatis is the term used by the great Reformation theologian and biblical exegete John Calvin to designate the sense of God's existence that seems to be endemic to the human race. He defined it as follows:

> There is within the human mind, and indeed by natural instinct, an awareness of divinity. This we take to be beyond controversy. To prevent anyone from taking refuge in the pretense of ignorance, God himself has implanted in all men a certain understanding of his divine majesty.[1]

Calvin believed that there was an intuitive aspect to man's nature that caused him to be capable of grasping the truth of God's existence from observations of the created realm around him. From the simplest of tribal groups to the most intelligent classes of people, the witness of God leaves no one without excuse. The fact of God's existence is, according to Calvin, immediately perspicuous to the human senses. There is no need for this belief to be delved through complicated syllogistic argument. It is immediate, not unlike the immediate knowledge of the existence of the material world or, for that matter, one's own existence. In a sense, the created world, or the perception thereof, triggers an immediate awareness of the divine in the human soul. The ubiquity of people groups who worship some form of deity gives testimony to the *sensus divinatis*. Calvin further elaborated the immediacy of the effect in the following words:

> We see that no long or toilsome proof is needed to elicit evidences that serve to illuminate and affirm the divine majesty; since the few we have sampled at random, withersoever you turn, it is clear that they are very manifest and obvious that they can easily be observed with the eyes and pointed out with the finger.[2]

What more effective trigger of this awareness of the divine could there be, but the recognition in natural phenomena of the qualities of beauty and awe? Standing beneath a towering range of mountains or witnessing the unearthly magnificence of a total solar eclipse or great comet, or the fearsome power of a thunderstorm, almost forces us to think of some power greater than ourselves. The very fact that most people groups throughout history have attributed theistic associations to such phenomena is surely proof of this. Of course, many have mistaken the phenomenon itself for the god, or ascribed what we might call a 'limited' god to specific phenomena, but even this admits of something that calls for our worship.

If the argument of the present book is correct, we now have scientific evidence for the connection between those features responsible for habitability and those that inspire the sense of beauty and awe awakening this intuition of the divine. Science may be said to have added a further dimension to our vision. Solar eclipses, polar lights and other beautiful and awe-inspiring phenomena are seen, not as 'gods' in themselves, but as parts of a wider tapestry that includes our own existence. The ability to recognize this surely constitutes part of what Calvin meant by *sensus divinatis*.

This doctrine of a capacity for awareness of the existence of God emerges in various forms in theological discussions. It is especially explicit in the teachings of mystics, Christian and otherwise. Amongst Christian mystics George Fox and his Quaker followers upheld the doctrine of the Inward Light (a sort of divine spark in the human soul) as a key belief. As evidence for the existence of the Inward Light, Fox and his followers pointed to the Prologue of the Gospel according to St. John and to the existence of conscience in the members of 'savage' tribes. Other Christian mystics, such as A. W. Tozer, spoke more of a spiritual analogue of the bodily senses, through which spiritual truth can be apprehended directly. Tozer, in particular, taught that the human spirit possessed senses just as the body possesses them and that in the same direct manner as we perceive material reality through the latter, so we directly perceive spiritual reality through the former.[3]

On the face of it, one may think that these doctrines (especially in the form presented by Fox) run foul of the Calvinistic doctrine of the total depravity of human nature, however it must be remembered that this term, as Calvin employed it, is a technical, theological, one which is not simply equated with its use in normal speech. It does not mean that human nature is depraved to the point of lacking any goodness. "Total" is used in the sense of implying the involvement of every part of human nature in corruption, not in the sense that the corruption *of* every part is absolute. There is no conflict in asserting that human nature is totally depraved in this technical sense, while at the same time maintaining that a certain degree of divine light may still be found within us. Indeed, if we were so depraved that all semblance of goodness had been eliminated, the existence of *sensus divinatis*, in any form, would be impossible. There would be nothing left within by which to recognize the presence of God.

Without delving into theological arguments, we may discern two aspects, not altogether separated, of *sensus divinatis*.

First, there is the inward aspect upon which mystics concentrate. In its weakest form, this amounts to little more than Immanuel Kant's appeal to the recognition of moral law within us as evidence for the existence of God. In the stronger sense as employed by Fox and Tozer, it amounts to a veiled perception of the presence of God himself.

Secondly, there is the sense of God's presence in creation.

Yet, the two are not intrinsically separate, as the presence of God in the created order is not perceived by the bodily senses, nor (according to Calvin) derived syllogistically from empirical data. It is directly apparent to something very like the inward spiritual senses of Tozer. We might even say that when, in prayer and meditation, the inward eye of the mystic "looks upon the divine", the awe and wonder produced by the intuition of deity floods the soul. Conversely, when the soul is flooded by these same emotions—albeit induced this time through the bodily perception of the grandeur of natural phenomena—the same set of psychological responses is recognized by the spiritual nature of man as a trigger to arouse (how ever slightly) the inward and spiritual senses.

It seems to me that a great number of thesis topics lie here just waiting for post-graduate theological students. Not only the relationship between the human sense of awe and appreciation of beauty and the doctrine of *sensus divinatis*, but also the more specifically theological issues such as how this doctrine of Calvin relates to those of Christian mystics such as Fox and Tozer, or even why this 'mystical' germ in Reformed Theology has been largely played down in favour of the more rationalistic approach taken by many contemporary Reformed Theologians. We remark that it was quite happily embraced by well known Calvinists of former ages, such as Jonathon Edwards and C. H. Spurgeon.

To pursue such matters would, however, take us far beyond the subject of this book.

Notes

1. John Calvin, *Institutes of the Christian Religion*, tr. Ford Lewis Battles, in the *Library of Christian Classics* vols. XX-XXI (Philadelphia: The Westminster Press, 1960), I. iii. I.
2. Ibid. I. v. 9.
3. A. W. Tozer, The Pursuit of God (Carlisle: OM Publishing, 1993), 53.

Appendix II
Transitive Complexity and Intentionality

The observation that certain more or less complex states of affairs possess the property that we have termed 'transitivity' raises an issue which will be familiar to anyone who has worked in the field of philosophy of mind. We refer to the property known as 'Intentionality'.

As employed by philosophers, this term is a technical one used to describe a particular characteristic of mental states that is very close to what we have been calling 'transitivity'. For example, a hope is a mental state that points beyond itself. It is not simply 'a hope' but a hope *for* something more or less definite. It may be a hope for something as specific as a fine day for the big football match or as broad as a hope for an easier life or a more peaceful world, but it cannot just be a hope totally devoid of object.

Similarly, perception must be perception of something. It is inherently relational; it cannot simply be perception without being perception *of* some object or state of affairs.

Nevertheless, this object or state of affairs to which a mental state is directed need not be something that actually exists. It may merely be a 'potential'. For example, one may hope that one receives a cheque for $100 in the mail tomorrow, but there is a good chance that this hope will be a vain one. However, it is no less a genuine hope, and no less an intentional mental state, for being vain.

It is here that mental states appear to differ from physical ones. Certainly, there are physical states that do relate to something beyond themselves in certain ways. A meteoroid travelling through space cannot simply collide: it must collide with *something*, such as the Moon's surface or the Earth's atmosphere. Yet the object of its collision must be an actual and material body. It cannot collide with a planet that does not exist, in the manner that we can hope for the arrival of a cheque that does not exist. Philosophers see this ability to be directed toward something which may not even exist as constituting the essence of Intentionality.

Philosophers of mind find the phenomenon of Intentionality interesting in so far as it superficially appears to provide a way of defining what we mean by a mental state. Physical states, they argue, do not exhibit this property.

For the concept of Intentionality to truly define what is meant by 'mental' however, philosophers must be able to demonstrate two things. They must show that no physical state can display Intentionality and they must demonstrate that *every* mental state has this characteristic.

In actual fact, both of these endeavours end in failure.

Looking at the last one first, it does appear pretty evident that there are states which we would undeniably classify as mental but which do not show the characteristic of Intentionality. An itch is one example. Certainly, the cause of this may be physical, but my conscious experience of it also makes it a mental state. But unlike, say, *hope*, the experience of an itch is not goal directed.

Moods form another class of mental states that may not necessarily be goal directed. A general feeling of happiness or of depression need not be related to anything in particular.

The advent of calculators and computers has also introduced a complication into the supposedly neat division between intentional mental and non-intentional physical states. If a computer—or a hand-held calculator for that matter—is calculating the square root of 493, it is performing an action that is directed toward a solution and which is identified by reference to that solution. In other words "calculating the square root of 493" is an intentional description. Moreover, if the computer is set to calculate the integral square root of 493, its calculation is directed toward something that does not exist.

For these reasons, Intentionality fails to provide a unique characterization of the mental. Many mental processes are intentional, but some are not. Most physical processes are not intentional, but a few are. Evidently, "Intentionality" and "mental" are not co-extensive terms; to the disappointment of many philosophers of mind.

On the other hand, Intentionality is important to the philosophy of mind in so far as it highlights a difficulty with theories purporting to identify mental states and processes with physical events in the brain and central nervous system. Such theories are known by the names of "Physicalism", "Identity Theory", "Central State Materialism" or, more generally, simply as "Materialism". The latter term can, however, also extend to less extreme theories in which mental states are understood, ephemeral products of brain states rather than being strictly identical with them. This moderate form of materialism is known as "Epiphenomenalism".

Physicalist theories however, equate mental states and brain states, without remainder. Therefore, it must logically follow that everything that can truthfully be said about a mental state must also be said about the corresponding cerebral state. After all, they are one and the same (in fact, even 'corresponding' is strictly speaking incorrectly used here. There are not two things which 'correspond', but one thing only).

Therefore, if Physicalism is correct, any cerebral state identifiable with an intentional mental one must *logically* be intentional also.

In fact, brain states do not present as intentional. Processes in the brain lack the type of goal direction required. Moreover, this difference in characterising mental and cerebral states is quickly seen as merely part of a far wider problem for the physicalist. The descriptions given to mental states on one hand and to physical (including cerebral) on the other, belong to entirely different categories. For example, suppose a patient complains of being in pain to his doctor. It is entirely fitting for the doctor to ask whether the pain is mild or severe, acute or dull, constant or fluctuating and so forth. Now let us suppose that the doctor succeeds in identifying the exact cerebral processes accompanying his patient's pain; that actually *constitute* his pain according to a physicalist. Can we suppose that the doctor would use the same terms to describe the cerebral processes he observes, as the patient uses to describe his pain?

Such a question comes across as little less than absurd. A pain, as experienced by one suffering it, might indeed be severe or dull, but what sense does it make to ask if the brain state accompanying this painful experience is severe or dull?

On the other hand, it is reasonable to think that the brain state has a particular colour, weight and length; that it involves a certain number of neurons and the like. But does this imply that the doctor should inquire as to the colour, weight and length of his patient's pain? Can we ask how many neurons the pain involves?

If both are describing the same thing without remainder, such questions may indeed be asked!

These considerations raise the issue of what Gilbert Ryle termed "Category Errors" or the erroneous description of a member of one category in terms correctly applicable only to a member of a different category. Ryle illustrates the error by the use of two simple examples.

In his first example, Ryle imagines a person, ignorant of the game of Cricket, mistakenly thinking that "team spirit" denotes another position in the game, on a par with bowler and batsman. One may imagine that somebody suffering from this confusion would not see the error in inquiring as to whether a tall or short man was better fitted to play team spirit!

Ryle's second example imagines a person being conducted over a university. After having been shown the various faculty buildings and residential colleges, he then asks to be taken to the university!

Clearly, the error of these two hypothetical individuals rests on their failure to distinguish the different categories involved. Members of a cricket team belong to one category, team spirit to another. One is a class of tangible human beings performing certain roles. The other is something intangible which is (hopefully!) shared by these team members.

Similarly, the university is not simply another building in addition to the faculty buildings, residential colleges, library and the like. It *is* this collection of buildings, plus the academic staff employed there and the entire academic fabric in which they participate.[1]

The same is true of mental and physical descriptions. We commit a category error if we try to describe brain states in terms suitable only for mental states and vice versa. Although there was a popular song in the late 1960s called *Love is Blue*, we do not literally believe that love has a colour. Nor does pain have a weight. The composer of *Love is Blue* was aware of this of course, and was not making a scientific statement through the title of the song. Yet to be consistent, the physicalist must do just that!

To get out of the corner in which he seems to be boxed, the physicalist is forced to distinguish between the cerebral states as known by subjective experience (where 'experience' words and intentional descriptions are valid) and external observation (where physical description alone is intelligible). This, however, takes him in the direction of the so-called Double Aspect theory of mind as well as raising the thorny problem of what "subjective experience" really means and what place it can have in a hard-line materialism. Already, Physicalism is beginning to crack.

Incidentally, this problem is not raised in the case of the computer making a calculation. We may observe the workings of the computer and quite justifiably describe them as intentional. The inner workings of the machine really are identical with the process of calculation, as no subjective experience is involved.

All of these issues are fascinating, but to pursue them further would lead us too far from the subject of this book. Questions raised by the philosophy of mind are, after all, just side issues in this context. Nevertheless, they have raised a very important matter which *is* of concern to our main thesis. That is to say, although Intentionality cannot be used to characterize mind per se, it does appear to characterize intelligent purpose. Mental states which lack Intentionality lack intelligent purpose. That is certainly not to say that they lack consciousness, or that their occurrence is not dependant upon 'Intelligence' in the wider sense. They simply do not display the property of being intelligently directed to something beyond themselves. On the other hand, the computer's process of calculation (although not conscious and not even the process of a living organism) is still 'intelligent' in the very basic sense of the word; the sense in which we can speak about 'artificial intelligence' without implying 'artificial mind'. Of course, we need not point out that a computer or calculator cannot even exist unless there is a human intelligence somewhere in the background.

In short, we suggest that where Intentionality is found, intelligence is evident, even though Intentionality fails to define mental activity per se.

We may say that intentional states possess a form of transitivity in so far as they point beyond themselves. We may note that transitive verbs are employed to express many of these mental states. Certain intentional states, however, are specifically directed toward the creation of states of affairs displaying Transitive Complexity in the sense in which we have been using that term.

Consider, once again, the now rather hackneyed example of an arrow painted on the floor of a parking station. This clearly did not 'just happen'. Somebody must have decided to place it there, determine where the best place for its location should be and then decide to go ahead and actually paint it at that spot. All of these steps involved mental states directed toward a definite goal. Moreover, the decisions themselves were made at a time when their immediate object (viz. the arrow) did not exist. These are clear instances of Intentionality.

Yet, although the arrow may have been the immediate goal toward which the decisions were directed, it was not the ultimate one. There existed the further goal (also having no concrete existence at the time the decisions were being made) of the smooth and safe operation of the parking lot. The arrow was not simply there for its own sake. As we have argued, its purpose was a transitive one; the purpose of enabling the parking lot to function without traffic chaos and accidents.

It seems to me that what we have been calling Transitive Complexity is really an 'extension' of the Intentionality possessed by the intelligent instigator of the process. Thus, the goal of safety and efficiency in the operation of the parking lot, as conceived in the minds of the architects and builders, finds concrete expression in the painted arrow; the coded message worked out in the mind of the mathematician becomes incarnate in the printed code, and the educator's desire to pass his knowledge onto others assumes material form as a text book.

If this line of argument is correct, TC can only be understood in terms of being the product of intelligence. If we are correct in arguing that intelligence is necessarily implied by Intentionality and if transitivity is effectively a product of Intentionality, transitivity and intelligence are therefore seen as necessarily connected.

We may then conclude that any state of affairs displaying TC cannot be adequately explained unless it is understood to have its origin in Intentionality and, ipso facto, intelligence. If a transitively complex state of affairs is found 'in nature', we see no reason why this requirement should be waived. Indeed, the logic is sufficiently tight to require an explanation which includes the presence of intelligence even in situations where human activity is clearly ruled out.

We see this as further strengthening our earlier conclusions regarding the presence of Intelligent Design in nature and the consequent necessity of postulating an Intelligent Designer.

Notes

1. Gilbert Ryle, *Intelligent The Concept of Mind* (Harmondsworth: Penguin, 1963), 17-24.

Index

A for Andromeda, 47, 48
absorption spectrum, 67
adenine, 51, 53
Airy, George, 66
Amalthea, 68, 81
amino acids, 48, 49, 50
ammonia, 69, 70
Anderson, Poul, 3, 16
angels, 89
annular eclipses, 64, 65
Anthropic Principle (AP), 6–12, 54
apes, 88
Aristotle, 5, 6
arrows, as evidence of design, 35, 37, 42, 43, 44, 45–47, 56, 57, 84, 104, 105, 118, 119
asteroids, 10, 23, 24, 69, 70, 72, 74, 78, 83, 94
astronomy, 18, 63, 97, 100
atmosphere
  of giant planets, 2, 11, 81, 82; of small planets, 11; of terrestrial planets, 15; of Venus, 2, 30; solar, 66, 67, 68 atmosphere of Earth, 16, 17, 18, 19, 23, 24, 65, 73, 74, 90, 92, 94, 95, 96, 97; clouds therein, 9; early, 19, 20, 23, 70–72; transparency of, 59, 77–78, 84
aurora, 73, 96–97, 98
avalanches, 91
awe, 87, 88, 89, 90, 91, 93, 95, 96, 97–99, 100, 101, 102, 104, 111, 112; points toward Transcendent Creator, 89, 113

B type stars, 10, 79
bacteria, 20, 50, 51, 52; flagellum of, 52
Barr, Stephen, 99, 107
A Beautiful Mind, 34
beauty, 59, 60, 61, 88, 89, 90, 92, 94, 97–103, 105, 111, 112; appreciation thereof, 60, 87, 103, 104, 108, 109, 113; "cosmic", 99–103; of laws of physics, 58, 98, 99, 100; of mathematics, 98, 99, 100; of universe, 13, 103, 104
Bell, Jocelyn, 45–46
Big Bang, 7, 13, 97, 105–108
biological luxuries, 61, 103, 104
birds, 88–89
Bondi, Herman, 12
Brownlee, Don, 63, 75

C type asteroids, 69, 70, 74
calendar, translation of ancient into modern, 69
Calvin, John, 111, 112, 113
carbon, 17, 30, 69, 70, 74, 88
carbon cycle, 17–18, 74
carbon dioxide (CO_2), 17, 18, 19, 20, 23, 74
carbonaceous meteorites, 70, 74
category errors, 117
central state materialism.
  See physicalism

cetaceans, 88
chance, 15, 26, 28, 30, 31, 35, 52, 57, 84
cromosphere, 65, 66, 67
coincidence(s), 10, 31, 61, 75, 77–84, 102, 104, 108; in apparent diameters of Sun and Moon, 1–19, 23, 29, 63, 64, 65
circumstellar habitable zone, 10
climate, 21, 68
clouds, 88, 89, 90, 91; dust, 73; giant molecular, 9, 10, 80; interstellar, 96, 97; non-water, 89; patterns in, 34, 36, 42–43, 55.
See also atmosphere of Earth
codes, 45–48, 75; genetic 37, 48–52; language as, 44
comets, 3, 9, 10, 14, 23, 69, 70, 72, 73, 74, 78, 80, 83, 93–96, 97, 98 Hale-Bopp, 73; Hyakutake, 94; Machholz, 72; Schwassmann-Wachmann, 73; Tempel-Tuttle, 95; Van Ness, 73
complexity, 15, 34, 35, 37, 40, 41, 42, 47, 48, 51, 52, 53, 59, 81, 82, 87, 101. *See also* irreducible complexity, specified complexity, transitive complexity
Comte, August, 67
consciousness, 101, 102, 104, 118
continents, 16, 17, 75; Pangaea, 75
Copernican Principle (CoP), 4–14, 87; and Anthropic Principle, 6–12; and Steady State cosmology, 13; misconceptions concerning, 5–6
corals, 18
coronagraph, 65, 66
corotation circle of galaxies, 9, 10
cosmic curiosity, 82, 83, 84, 87, 99, 100, 103, 104, 108, 109
Cosmological Principle (CP), 12
Crab Nebula, 96
Crick, Francis, 48
crust; of Earth, 15, 16, 17, 18, 21, 23, 24, 27, 74, 76; of Mars & Venus, 16
Curie point, 76
cyanobacteria, 20
cytosine, 48, 50

Darwin, Charles, 88
Darwinian evolution. *See* natural selection
Davies, Paul, 109
Dawkins, Richard, 34, 37, 40, 84
days: length of and temperature, 21; effect of Moon upon, 21, 22, 24, 25
deoxyribose phosphate, 48
Dembski, William, 35–37, 40, 42, 44, 105
density waves, 8
Descartes, Rene, 39
design, viii, 31, 34, 35, 46, 51, 52, 55, 57, 58, 60, 84, 99, 105, 109, 119; characteristics of, viii, 35–45, 46; evidence for, 53–55
Design Hypothesis, viii, ix
designoids, 34, 38, 41
deuterium, 69
distances: Earth-Sun, 2, 19, 20, 63, 64; of fixed stars, 5–6; of Moon, 19, 25, 63, 64; determination of cosmic, 78–79, 96
Dias, W. S., 9
DNA, 48–52
double aspect theory of mind, 118
dust, 50, 89, 94; impacts, 73; interstellar, 7, 80

Earth, viii, 1, 50; age of, 105; as alien's nursery, 53; as 'platform of observation', 78–79, 81, 84, 87, 89; changing attitudes toward, 2, 63; early beliefs about, 5–6; fine-tuned condition on, 53, 54, 77, 99, 103, 104, 105, 108; in Solar System, 69, 73, 74, 78; interior of, 75, 91; magnetic field of, 73–73, 76, 97–97; not a typical planet, 2, 3, 4, 14, 15–31, 59, 63, 65, 87, 105; position in Galaxy, 9–10, 80; rotation of, 68. *See also* atmosphere of Earth; crust of Earth; orbit of Earth
earthquakes, 21, 75, 91; and knowledge of Earth's interior, 75–76; and sense of awe, 91–92
earthshine, 6
eclipses: perfect, 18, 23,

63–69, 81; solar, 23, 93; super, 64, 68
Edwards, Jonathan, 113
Einstein, Albert, 12, 13, 68, 98
elements, 7, 8, 10, 17, 26, 50, 67, 80, 81, 96, 97
elliptical galaxies: dwarf, 8; giant, 11
emission spectrum, 67
energy, 11, 21, 24, 25, 81, 89, 96, 106
epiphenomenalism, 116
exo-planets, 3
extraterrestrial life, 1, 108
extraterrestrial intelligence, 45, 46, 47; pulsar mistaken for, 45–46

'Face on Mars', 36, 43–44
Fegley, Bruce, 71
fine tuning, 53, 54, 55, 58, 76, 80, 82
First Cause, 104
flash spectrum, 67
Flew, Anthony, 53
Fox, George, 112, 113

galactic habitable zone, 9, 10
galaxies, 4, 8, 11, 50, 79, 80, 96, 97, 98, 105, 107.
Galileo, 6
gambler's fallacy, 56
gas giants (planets), 3, 16
General Relativity, theory of, 12, 68
giant molecular clouds. *See* clouds, giant molecular,
glaciers, 20, 68, 91
glories, 90–91
God, 56; as Designer, 105; glory of, 89, 109
God and Philosophy, 53
Gold, Thomas, 12
Gonzalez, Guillermo, 63, 64, 65, 68, 75, 77, 80, 81, 87, 90, 93, 97
gravity, 40, 55, 65; Newton's Theory of, 98
greenhouse effect, 19–20
guanine, 48, 50

habitability: of Earth, 15, 17, 21, 23, 25, 27 – 29; requirements for, 9, 10, 29, 30, 54, 58, 69, 77, 81, 82, 84, 88, 89, 90, 91, 94, 96, 97, 105
Hadean Era, 71

Haldane, J.B.S., 101
heavy elements. *See* metals
Heinlein, Robert, 15
Heisenberg Uncertainty Principle, 106, 108
Heisenberg, Werner, 108
helium, 7, 67
HEOS-2, 73

Herschel, William, 27, 28, 66
Hewish, Anthony, 45, 46
Hoyle, Fred, 46, 47, 51, 101, 104
Hubble Space Telescope, 73, 79, 80
Huxley, Aldous, 60
hydrogen, 2, 7, 17, 56, 65, 69, 70
hydrological cycle, 74

ice, 17, 20, 69, 70, 74, 89
identity theory of mind. *See* physicalism
impacts: dust, 73; giant primordial on Earth, 23–27; meteorite, 9, 15, 30; on Mercury and Uranus, 26–27
Inflation, theory of, 105
intelligence, viii, 34, 37, 38, 44, 47, 51, 53, 60, 84, 104, 108, 118, 119
Intelligent Design Movement, 51
intentionality, 115, 116, 118, 119
introns, 49
Inward Light, 112
irreducible complexity, 52
isotopes, of oxygen, 71

James, William, 92
Janssen, Pierre Jules Cesar, 67
jovian planets, 15. *See also* jupiters
Jupiter, 11, 16, 69, 78, 79, 81, 89; life on, 1, 2, 28, 82; moons of, 64, 68, 81
jupiters, 3, 96; hot, 10

Kant, Immanuel, 112
Kirschvink, J., 19, 20
Kopp, R., 19
Kuiper Belt, 25

lakes, 74, 78
Laskar, J., 22
laws of physics, 54, 55, 58, 81,

82, 98, 99, 100, 103, 104, 106; originating in Big Bang, 106–107
Leonid meteor shower, 95
Lepine, J. R. D., 9
'LGM-1', 45
lightning and thunder, 88–90
life, 17, 30, 48-55, 57, 58, 59, 60, 65, 69–75, 77, 88, 90, 94; 'life chauvinism', 26; on other planets, 1–6, 46, 63; solar, 27–28, 66; terrestrial, 6–12, 15, 16, 17, 19, 20, 21, 2, 23, 25, 27–29, 64, 65, 78, 79, 80, 82, 87, 89, 91, 93, 97, 99, 104, 105
Local Group of galaxies, 11
Lockyer, Joseph Norman, 67
luminosity of stars, 79
Lyot, Bernard, 65

magnetism, 76, 97
magnetic fields, 11, 16, 23, 45, 74, 76–77, 94, 96, 97; as protectors of life, 11, 16, 21, 76, 77, 96
Mariner 4, 3
marine sediments, 76
Mars, 1, 2, 3, 14, 15, 16, 17, 23, 27, 28, 30, 34, 69, 77; life on, 1, 2, 11. *See also* Face on Mars
Marsden, Brian, 72
mediocrity premise. *See* Principle of Mediocrity
megaverse, 55–58
Mercury, 1, 3, 11, 16, 26, 27, 79
Messier, Charles, 98
metabolism, 20
metals (heavy elements), 7, 8, 10, 11, 80, 96, 97
meteors, 94–95
meteorites, 94–95
methane, 17, 19, 20, 70, 89
Milky Way, 4, 6, 7, 8, 10, 11, 79, 80
Miller, Stanley, 70
Miller-Urey Process, 70–71, 74, 89
Milne, E. A., 81
mind, philosophy of, 115, 116, 118
minerals, 18
molecules, 16, 17, 30, 47, 48, 49, 70, 73, 81, 94, 96
moods, 116
Moon, 2, 3, 6, 11, 16, 18, 19, 20–26, 27, 29, 63, 64, 65, 67, 68, 69, 93
moons, 16, 17, 19, 64
mountains, 88, 90–91, 100; and plate tectonics, 16; as abode of gods, 90, 91; on Sun, 67
Mount Rushmore, 36, 37
Mount Wingen, 33, 34
mystics, 112–113

nanotechnology, 48
naturalism, 53
natural selection, 37, 52, 83, 84, 102, 108, 109
Neptune, 25

neutron stars, 45. *See also* pulsars
Newton, Isaac,
Nirenberg, M., 49
Nitrogenous compounds, 89
"nothing", ambiguity in the word, 107–108
nucleotides, 48–50
numinous, 101, 102, 104

O Type stars, 10, 81
oliquity of Earth's axis, 22, 24
ocean(s), 74, 77, 88, 90, 92
Oort Cloud, 9
ordinary chondrites, 71
organic molecules, 70, 73, 94
oxygen, 17, 19, 20, 56, 74, 88; isotopes of, 71

parallax, stellar, 78–79
pattern(s), 34, 35, 36, 37, 43, 45, 54; of magnetic reversals, 76; of recognition, 34
Perfect Cosmological Principle (PCP), 12–14
perfect solar eclipses. *See* eclipses, perfect
photons, 96, 106
photosphere, of Sun, 18, 65, 66, 67
photosynthesis, 17, 20
physics, laws of. *See* laws of physics
physicalism, 116–118
planets, types of, 3, 16
planetesimals, 24
plate tectonics, 10, 16, 17, 74, 75, 76, 90, 91
Platonic Ideal, 106

Pluto, 25
pollen, 88
Principle of Mediocrity (PoM), 4, 5, 13
The Privileged Planet, 59
Privileged Planet Hypothesis (PPH), 63, 65
probability, 4, 8, 9, 30, 35, 42, 51, 56, 57, 78, 107
Ptolemy, 5–6
pulsars, 46
purpose, of existence, 87, 104, 105, 109
Puthoff, Harold, 108

quantum leaps of complexity, 52
quantum vacuum, 106, 107, 108

radiation, 2, 9, 10, 16, 70, 76, 77, 80, 83, 89, 94, 105
rainbows, 67, 90, 91, 97,
Rare Earth, 63
The Rare Earth Hypothesis, 63
rationality, 6
resonance, 22, 24
RNA, 49–50
ribosomes, 47
Richards, Jay, 63, 64, 75, 77, 80, 81, 87, 90, 97
rock(s), 18, 20, 25, 26, 27, 33, 34, 35, 36, 40, 70, 71, 74, 76
rotation, of Earth and planets, 20, 21, 22, 23, 24, 25, 26, 68
Ryle, Gilbert, 117

St. John, prologue to gospel of, 112
Sandwell, David, 76, 77
Saturn, 2, 17, 22, 89
Schaefer, Laura, 71
Schroedinger, Erwin, 108
sedimentation, 74
seismographs, 75
Sekanina, Zdenek, 73
sensus divinatis, 111 - 113
SETI, (Search for Extraterrestrial Intelligence), 45
shellfish, 18
silicates, 18
silicon, 30, 69
snowball Earth, 19–20, 23

SOHO (Solar and Heliospheric Observatory), 66, 72
solar wind. *See* wind, solar
space, 1, 2, 4, 6, 11, 12, 16, 17, 23, 27, 28, 29, 46, 47, 66, 67, 68, 70, 73, 79, 80, 83, 94, 95, 98, 101, 106, 107
specification, 36, 42
Specified Complexity, 35, 37, 40, 44, 105
spectrum, 65, 66, 67, 97
spectrohelioscope, 67
spectroscope, 65, 66, 67, 97
spiral galaxies,
spiritual sense(s), 112
Spurgeon, C. H., 113
standard candles, 79
sprites, 90
stars, 2, 3, 4, 5, 6, 7 – 12, 15, 25, 26, 27, 45, 46, 47, 50, 65, 66, 67, 68, 78, 79, 80, 91, 96, 97, 98, 100, 105
Steady State Cosmology, 13,
sulfur, 30, 33, 69
Sun, 2, 3, 6, 7, 9–11, 16, 18, 19, 20, 21, 23, 24, 25, 26, 27, 28, 29, 45, 50, 69, 70, 72, 77, 78, 79, 80, 91, 95, 96, 98. *See also* eclipses, solar; photosphere of
sunspots, 67
supernovas, 7, 9, 10, 80, 96, 97

Taylor, Richard, 38
Taylor, Stuart, 26
temperature, 2, 18, 19–23, 65, 71, 74, 75, 76, 79, 93
terrestrial planets, 3, 10, 16, 17, 25, 26, 71, 96
Thales of Miletos, 83
theories, as existing independently of mind, 99
thunderstorms, 89, 90
thymine, 48, 50
tides, 21, 22, 25, 65, 68, 71
time, Big Bang as origin of, 107
Titan, 2, 17, 21, 89
tomography, three-dimensional, 75
Tozer, A. W., 113
Transitive Complexity, 39–48, 54, 60, 82, 84, 104–105, 118–119

Triton, 25
tsunami, 75
Tunguska event, 78
Twain, Mark, 72

ultraviolet radiation, 2, 70, 77
universals, 106
universe, VII, VIII, IX, 4, 5, 6, 7, 8, 11, 12, 13, 14, 15, 27, 29, 46, 48, 50, 51, 53–60, 63, 65, 67, 69, 78, 79, 80–82, 84, 87, 89, 93, 96, 97, 98, 99, 100, 101, 103–109
uracil, 49
Uranus, 26, 27, 66
Urey, Harold, 70

vacuum fluctuations, 107–108
Venus, 1, 2, 3, 14, 15, 16, 17, 19, 21, 23, 24, 26, 30, 69, 78, 96
volcanism, 17, 23, 24, 74
volcanoes, 18, 33, 34, 77, 90

Waltham, Dave, 22–23
Ward, Peter, 63, 75
water, 2, 9, 16, 17, 18, 20, 21, 30, 34, 36, 40, 41, 56, 69, 70, 71, 74, 75, 77, 89, 90, 94
waterfalls, 90
water world(s), 17, 21, 90
Watson, James D, 48
Watson, Lyall, 92
Weyl, Hermann, 99
Wickramasinghe, Chandra, 51
wind, 34, 35, 36, 42, 91; solar, 11, 16, 21, 94
Wingen Maid, 34, 36, 37, 44

X-rays, emitted by lightning, 90

Young, Charles A, 67
young-Earth creationism, 105

zircons, 71
zitterbewegung, 108

About the Author

David A. J. Seargent earned his MA and PhD in Philosophy from the University of Newcastle in the Australian state of New South Wales and for several years lectured in that subject with the University's adult education department. He has also tutored/lectured within the Philosophy Department, including a lecture series for honours and postgraduate students on the philosophy of universals.

Long interested in Astronomy, Dr. Seargent has been an active amateur astronomer for many years and has made several contributions to the observations of comets, including the discovery of a comet in 1978, which now bears his name. He acted as the Australian co-ordinator for visual observations of Halley's Comet during its most recent return in 1986, as part of the International Halley Watch program. He continues to contribute comet observations to the International Comet Quarterly data base and is a regular contributing editor of the popular astronomy magazine Australian Sky and Telescope.

Dr. Seargent is the author of numerous articles and several books, including *Comets: Vagabonds of Space* (1983), a popular account for amateur astronomers and interested laypeople, and an academic treatise *Plurality and Continuity: An Essay in G. F. Stout's Theory of Universals*.

He lives with wife Meg at The Entrance, north of Sydney in New South Wales.

www.ingramcontent.com/pod-product-compliance
Lightning Source LLC
Chambersburg PA
CBHW030116010526